The Proletarian Handbook

Joseph Waters

CONTENTS

PART FOUR: MISCELLANEA

Introduction

This book is a compilation of eight years of my blog, Proletarian Center for Research, Education and Culture; or Prole Center for short. This is a selection of blog entries and tidbits that should help elucidate the political situation of the United States and the world. It is a result of the thinking, accumulated wisdom, and some speculations, of one who has spent well over a decade researching, pondering and analyzing how the world really works, who runs the show, and what ought to be done about it.

The chapters are mostly brief and originally appeared, for the most part, as independent blog entries and/or articles published on some other online news source. Some of the writings that are several years old or more have dates included to show the evolution in my thinking or to otherwise provide historical context.

The book is categorized into four parts based on subject area and the chapters can be read in any order, but readers who are not well-versed in political theory, particularly Marxist theory, might be well-served to begin with Part One.

Joseph Waters of Prole Center

www.prolecenter.wordpress.com

People always have been the foolish victims of deception and self-deception in politics, and they always will be until they have learnt to seek out the interests of some class or other behind all moral, religious, political and social phrases, declarations and promises.

- Vladimir Ilyich Lenin

Part One: Political Theory & Political Ideologies

Chapter 1: The Difference Between Liberals and Conservatives in America

Liberals and conservatives represent two factions of the bourgeoisie. These factions are both adherents of the same ideology of classical liberalism or capitalism. While these factions are not necessarily strictly tied to a political party, to simplify things overall it could be said that liberals tend to be Democrats, and as such, are essentially right-wing, moderate conservatives. The far-right, ultra-conservatives types, on the other hand, tend to align themselves with the Republican party.

The difference between the right and the far right is simply this: The far right believes its own bullshit. A right wing (liberal) bourgeois will lie and connive and not necessarily believe everything he or she says in order to get their way, but a far right-winger is crazy. They actually do believe things like Americans are God's chosen people, black people are genetically inferior and that climate change is a hoax.

The former group are actually conservatives since they want to preserve the status quo of bourgeois liberalism, or capitalism operating under a façade of democracy. The latter should really be considered ultra-conservatives (or far right) since they want to roll the clock *back* and return to the status-quo ante. Another term for these folks is *reactionary*. The far right has open disdain for any pretense of democracy, and despite their protestations at the accusation, they really prefer something very closely resembling a fascist form of government.

Genuine liberals (who believe what they say) are fanatic in their belief in bourgeois democracy, a very superficial and self-serving interpretation of basic human rights that they have called "civil rights" and their "humanitarian" interventions to supposedly promote these things abroad – which is really just trying to put a human face on naked aggression and imperialist expansion.

Genuine conservatives (who believe what they say) are also fanatic in their beliefs in religion, the supernatural, tribalism and white supremacy.

Both of these two wings of the same bird of prey work in tandem to bamboozle the masses and keep them under control. The conflict between them is largely Kabuki theater or akin to professional wrestling. Coke or Pepsi – take your pick.

Chapter 2: The Role of the Nominally Left in the US

April 19, 2011

To begin with, I'd like to state quite clearly as I feel it necessary to do again and again, that there really is no Left in the U.S. at this time. What passes for a Left in this country is fully tied in to the establishment. Its job is to provide an outlet for venting frustration with the system by criticizing and protesting against it, but essentially doing nothing constructive to fundamentally change it. The "Left" leaders carefully herd dissent into safe avenues that they can control such as electioneering, petitions, legislation, litigation and even recall referendums. Eventually some small reforms may materialize, but nothing that will go nearly far enough to dismantle unjust systems of power and privilege.

To give an example, consider the following slogan heard from an anonymous Left leader at a rally in Wisconsin recently: "Put down those posters and pick up those clipboards." Apparently there is a campaign to recall Gov. Walker of Wisconsin for his attacks on public-sector workers. As the quote above illustrates, the job for Democratic politicians and bought-out union bosses is to make sure the workers go back to work; they will do all in their power to discourage and prevent a General Strike, which is just what is needed. The Left establishment understands very well that this type of direct action could be powerfully effective, much more so than gathering signatures to remove Gov. Walker so he can just be replaced by a Democrat who will essentially do the same thing. The only difference is that a Democrat will likely be willing to compromise a little, whereas the Republicans compromise not at all. The truth of the situation is that workers should not compromise or give one inch; their backs are already against the wall!

One more telling example of the way in which the Democrats (remember, not a true Left, but only nominally Left charlatans) screw over the working class is by appealing to the legislative process, procedures and formalities of political conduct – things that have to be done just the right way by the experts who are our so-called representatives. I give below an excerpt of a speech given at the Wisconsin legislature by Rep. Roys after the Republicans quickly, sneakily and illegally slammed through the anti-worker legislation there about two months ago:

"It appears that illegal action was taken. Action started happening before the time that we were even scheduled to be in this body. We had members that were asking to be recognized; they were not recognized. This morning, that happened again. That is outrageous, and it is not worthy of us. It's not worthy of any one of you. For some of you over there, your hearts are breaking, too, because you don't want to do business this way. None of us wants to see this institution and this state take that direction. This is the United States of America. We will disagree passionately. We will raise our voices. We will protest. We will be peaceful. But by God, by God, we will give each other a basic level of respect and human dignity when we disagree. You can win on this, but do not win this way. Do not win this way. I beg of you, reconsider. You will win the vote. Strike the previous action. Let's do this the right way. You can still do the wrong thing, but please, please, look in your hearts. Let's do it the right way. Thank you."

Yep, she really said that. You can still do the wrong thing, just do it the right way. When you cheat to get your way we will be peaceful and passive and just bitch and moan and stand on principle. Let's follow procedure, which is more important than the substance of our disagreement. Do the wrong thing, but for the love of god, just do it the right way. Readers, I hope I do not have to elaborate any more on the embarrassing ridiculousness and insanity of those remarks. Never forget, politicians, like business leaders, even labor leaders unfortunately at the present time, are nothing more than professional liars and charlatans. We need real, genuine leaders who unequivocally stand for the working class; and we need an educated, empowered rank-and-file that can recognize the difference between an opportunist charlatan and the real McCoy.

Chapter 3: The Liberal Media and the Plot to Move the Country Further Right

Much of the media is liberal, but not in the sense of being left-wing as the American far right maintains.

From the very beginning of the so-called Cold War there were lurid tales promulgated of an international communist conspiracy. Teachers, university professors, Hollywood filmmakers and actors, artists, writers, and of course the "liberal media" were all a part of this vast conspiracy; it seemed that the communists had infiltrated every sector of American society, and especially those dealing with the news and entertainment media, education and culture.

However, when it comes to the idea of the so-called liberal media supposedly trying to help prepare the way for a communist takeover, I believe this narrative, like so much else in America, is upside-down. And yes, right-wingers are still very much convinced of this communist takeover, although they often now refer to it as the new world order (NWO) or the globalists, collectivists, Illuminati, etc. – same basic idea.

The mainstream or liberal news media preaches to an increasingly smaller and smaller choir. By all accounts they have rock-bottom ratings and yet they persist in doing the same thing. Like Trump of today, the mainstream media (MSM) also gave plenty of coverage in the 90's to presidential candidate, and "former" KKK imperial wizard, David Duke, without directly challenging his racist past which he claimed to have abandoned. The MSM enabled David Duke, just as they enabled Trump, through sensationalism. It's a case of reverse psychology. What happens when you tell someone: Whatever you do, don't look, don't go there, don't do that!? They do the opposite, almost out of instinct or an innate sense of morbid curiosity. Remember the old Hollywood adage: There's no such thing as bad publicity.

There appears to be a contrived US left-right debate formula: Liberals (the fake left) consistently make fun of and condescend the conservatives and then you get a continual backlash and the conservatives just dig in their heels and double down on their craziness. You had the same hostility and vicious mockery from liberals and Democrats toward Bush Jr. through entertainment media with shows like That's My Bush, Lil' Bush, The Daily Show, Bill Maher, etc. This continues today. The result is that the US "left" (which is really centrist at best), along with left ideas as filtered through these liberals, become further alienated and the country as a whole moves further to the right.

Chapter 4: Most of Us Are Not Middle Class

Most of us are not members of the middle class. This is one of the most awful and damaging myths that have been propagated by the ruling class. Take a look at the excerpt below from a U.S. Congressional committee hearing where members of the ruling class, or their fully vetted and most trusted representatives, talk among themselves about social class. They are discussing Pakistan in this instance, but the same applies to the U.S. population and anywhere else in the world.

Committee Chairman, Rep. John Tierney (D-MA): I guess part of my point was, you know, we have a situation over there now where **the middle class — lawyers, judges, the business people, or whatever** [emphasis mine] — seem to be on one side of the fence, and the military establishment on the other.

And I would guess that we have to be real careful about whether or not we side with the people of Pakistan, or are perceived to be siding with or against them on this. And it's going to be a real delicate use of smart power in that situation.

Former Deputy Secretary of State, Richard Armitage: I think the question of Pakistan is so complicated. You're right: **People seem**

to be on one side — and the military, and I would say the elite, on the other side [emphasis mine] with President Musharraf.[1]

Apparently, the elites who own and run Pakistan are not being sufficiently pliant and subservient to U.S. elites; therefore, the U.S. ruling class is scheming to divide and conquer by pitting the Pakistani middle class against the ruling class. The Pakistani working class will be used as pawns in this "great game" but will receive no benefit should the U.S. establishment succeed in its schemes. If successful, the U.S. will elevate a few members of the Pakistani middle class to elite status under its control and the rest of the middle class will materially benefit to some appreciable degree; once again, you can be sure that the working class will get the shaft.

It is important to understand that to be middle class is to be affluent. Also note from the above exchange that these upper class folks refer only to the middle class as "the people"; the rest of us are not considered to be people – we're tools, we're trash, we're expendable. Just as under chattel slavery the slaves were not considered to be human or at least not fully human, under wage slavery (capitalism) the rulers don't consider wage slaves to be fully human.

Middle class people are often millionaires or close to it. They make up no more than 20% of the population. The upper class/elites/ruling class are the infamous 1%. Then you have your approximately 80% of the rest of the population that is working class; this includes the destitute, the poor, the not-so-poor, and those who live reasonably comfortably, but who would be in big trouble with the loss of a couple of paychecks or if confronted with a major illness. The economic and moral interests of these classes are diametrically opposed. The bulk of the American middle class always has, and probably always will, side with the upper class when push comes to shove. What is good for this group, collectively known as the bourgeoisie, is bad for the working class and vice versa.

Chapter 5: A Brief Glimpse into the Bourgeois Mentality

On RT News a few years ago, there was a documentary called "Kilimanjaro Challenge" where they apparently document disabled folks trying to climb up one of the tallest mountains in the world. This is meant to be incredibly inspiring. I have a question, though. Why? Why bother? Why do they want to climb this huge mountain? What do they feel they have to prove? This is not inspiring, it's silly. I believe this is a bourgeois type of mentality where one feels the need to always accomplish something, especially something challenging or competitive, regardless of need or even when it serves absolutely no purpose at all, aside from bragging rights.

I have a message to these people: Hey guys, stay off the mountain. Write a children's book. Get involved in your local community. Mentor a kid. Clean up a park. Those would be much more meaningful ways to spend your time and effort.

I didn't become a socialist so disabled people could climb up one of the tallest mountains in the world limping the entire way, or worse, crawling on their knuckles. This is ridiculous!

Chapter 6: Bourgeois Internationalism under American Leadership

As I have noted many times on my blog, there is a very large degree of class consciousness and class solidarity among the international bourgeoisie. This is what the far right ultra-nationalist maniacs interpret as "globalism" or a "new world order." Washington (or New York City, if you like) is the hub and capital of the cross-border bourgeois nation. The U.S. is where the bourgeoisie of other countries come running and crying when the proletariat (working class) begin to take control of the economic system and the political reins of power.

When they are not directly competing with each other, the bourgeoisie can display a great deal of solidarity and commiseration; and they will even frankly confide in each other. What they will tell their class comrades they would never willingly reveal to their class enemies, the proletariat.

I was recently made privy to a conversation among several illustrious card-carrying bourgeois businessmen from the U.S., Russia and the Ukraine. The American, after listening to his Slavic counterparts express their intense loathing for President Vladimir Putin of the Russian Federation, inquired why they hated him so much. "What, specifically, has he done that you don't like?" he wanted to know. "How has he injured you?"

The American businessman, despite his class status and his American citizenship, is actually a decent sort of a guy. He at least seemed none too eager to believe all the terrible things he was told by the mainstream media about Putin and about Russia.

The Russian businessmen, along with their Ukrainian friend, did not hesitate in their answer. At this point, some naive souls might imagine that the reason for their distaste was that Putin was not very nice to gay people. Or, that he was cracking down on the political opposition; or perhaps he was infringing on the Russian people's inherent civil and human rights. If you guessed that any of these were the reason for these oligarchs' hatred of Putin then you are dead wrong. The answer that was readily given was thus:

"That motherfucker won't let us take our money out of Russia!!"

Apparently, President Putin and his government had figured out a way to stop capital flight out of Russia. However, presumably, he would allow these *gentlemen* to invest their money in Russia; but this particular act of curtailing capital flight, (a common, and one of the first to be used, methods of economic sabotage) and this alone, was enough to earn Putin the eternal enmity of these Russian oligarchs – for they were verified by the trusted source who related the tale to be, if not billionaires, then at least multi-multi-millionaires.

So, there you have it. Despite all the bullshit propaganda, what it comes down to is this: President Vladimir Putin, though not the Soviet-style communist some of us would like him to be, is however a populist nationalist and anti-imperialist. He is looking after the interests of average, every-day Russian citizens (in other words, the Russian proletariat). Unlike a socialist, he also protects the interests of the Russian petty bourgeoisie and even those oligarchs who "play by the rules" and support the Russian state. For this, President Putin is demonized in the Western media and his country is under assault by various covert and not-so-covert means in order to effect regime change – to overthrow him and replace him with a more pliant and servile vassal of the U.S. Empire.

Chapter 7: Are You Primarily a Consumer or a Worker?

Depends on who you ask.

I saw a crypto-currency fanatic and right-wing libertarian on TV say that people are primarily, and firstly, consumers. This is something I have heard a lot from these types. Bourgeois right-wing libertarians are absolutely *obsessed* with currency and with consumer choice. This attitude indicates someone with significant privilege, and too much money and leisure time. Most Americans spend the bulk of their time working and have relatively little disposable income.

People often don't recognize their own biases, but Freudian slips like the aforementioned will often reveal them to you if you pay close attention. Political activism that revolves around donations to charities and NGO's, economic boycotts or other questions of how and where to spend your money are sure signs of a bourgeois mentality that will in no way challenge the capitalist system. (Elections are another worthless exercise, by the way, but that is a whole other story.) Buying gold and bitcoin is another non-option and dead end in the pursuit of working class emancipation.

Chapter 8: Shills for a "Pure" Capitalism

In an RT clip advertising the Kaiser Report, Max explains how society is changing and people are moving away from solely individual self-interest and toward more concern for their fellow citizens, their "network" as he called it. Max realized that what he described was akin to socialism and so he quickly pointed out at the end of his comments that "this is not socialism because socialism has failed." No proof is given; at least not in this short segment.

If it can be said that socialism failed (notwithstanding there still being socialist countries in existence and others moving in that direction; namely, China, Cuba, North Korea, Venezuela, Bolivia, Eritrea, South Africa to name a few) we must ask *why* did it fail? The presumption is that the Soviet Union, the pillar of socialism, failed all on its own because its system was critically flawed and inefficient.

There is much more to the story, but the short version is this: The capitalist West, led by the United States, did in fact defeat the Soviet Union and the socialist countries of eastern Europe. They did this through the use of the CIA (whose mission it was to destroy communism covertly since a direct military conflict would be mutually destructive) by employing sabotage, propaganda, psychological warfare, subversion, economic sanctions and other covert means. Socialism suffered a major defeat with the collapse of the USSR, but is now on the rise once again. Can it defeat the evil U.S. Empire this time? Only time will tell.

But one thing I can tell you for sure is that Max Keiser is full of shit. He is a shill, in a long line of shills and pundits going back over 100 years who have clamored for a return to the "real" capitalism that was good and fair. The kind of capitalism where small business could thrive. This kind of capitalism only exists in the imagination of the petty bourgeoisie who simply cannot understand, or as Lenin would say *pretend not to understand,* that the amalgamation of capital into a financial plutocracy where billionaire bankers rule – this effect of the capitalism system that has come into being – is the very result that was inevitable and understood by those who played the game to win. If you tore everything down and started capitalism all over again, you would eventually get the same result, or something very similar, once again. As George Orwell said in his review of the godfather of right-wing, market libertarianism Friedrich Hayek's book, *The Road to Serfdom:*

" . . . he [Hayek] does not see, or will not admit, that a return to 'free' competition means for the great mass of people a tyranny probably worse, because more irresponsible, than that of the State. The trouble with competitions is that somebody wins them. Professor

Hayek denies that free capitalism necessarily leads to monopoly, but in practice that is where it has led . . ."[2]

Max Keiser does not see, or will not admit that a so-called return to the "pure" capitalism of his fevered dreams would not lead to the social justice, egalitarianism and freedom that he claims to desire. We've seen this act before and we know how it ends.

Chapter 9: Profile of an Ultra Right-Wing Libertarian

The following is a comment I found on Alex Jones' Info Wars website. It provides a good profile of far right-wing American libertarians who at times attempt to present themselves as populists, but are in fact off the charts ultra-conservative psychos. These are the "gun nuts" and the new world order conspiracy theorists. I have outlined in red certain words and phrases that are quite revealing signs of an ultra right-winger. Whenever you encounter two or three, or more, of these themes you will know that you are dealing with a bona fide fascist. The following example is pretty obvious since he or she uses practically all of the far right themes as well as being quite explicit in message. Others won't be quite this obvious, especially if you are speaking with them face to face. They will probably be much more calm and polite, and use some populist and fairly progressive language, but if you keep them talking long enough these themes, or memes, will start to leak out. Behold the craziness:

"The fbi are the masters of terror domestically, second only to the cia internationally, the <u>Department of Human Sacrifice</u>* are the new kids on the block – but with much more control into every aspect of <u>We, the People</u>'s lives. <u>Race War</u> is their ultimate goal to get the unstoppable ball rolling for <u>complete takeover</u>. The time grows nigh. Their plans are terror – to wage a war of terror on US

soil. Ferguson is the beginning. The <u>evil satanic powers</u> that be will now begin their reign of terror. Prepare accordingly. They are bringing in their <u>black jungle muscle</u> from all over the country. LE* is being used by dh<u>STASI</u>*, the fbi and doj* to divide and try and conquer. LE, you had better realize just who your enemies are. It sure as heck AINT your fellow citizen. dhSTASI and the <u>child rapists</u> that control DC and the federal agencies are your enemy, they are our enemy – you, LEO's* are being played and set up, you will be   cannon   fodder…"
<u>LoneWolf</u>

LE/O = law enforcement/officer; doj = dept. of justice; dept. of human sacrifice/dhSTASI = dept. of homeland security – the author

Here is my quick and dirty analysis of LoneWolf's message who no doubt considers himself a libertarian:

1) Using the phrase "We, the People" – straight from the U.S. constitution. (Conservatives consider this to literally be a sacred document.) Leftists (not fake leftists or liberals) would use terms like, "the people," "the masses," "the workers," or "proletarians."

2) The writer invokes the supernatural and religion, and not as a metaphor. The ruling elite is generally described as not only evil (which they clearly are), but as "demonic" or "satanic."

3) Libertarians seem to deny or else are truly baffled by the concept of socioeconomic classes and a struggle between classes. In their view, most rich people are good. Of course, there are exceptions that prove the rule, but most rich people in the sense especially of the power elites who sit on corporate boards and in government are bad guys because of their socioeconomic class position; their wealth is the proof of their wickedness. At any rate, wicked or not (as you like), they clearly use their tremendous wealth to dominate and enslave the rest of us. Libertarians have no real problem with this because they are mostly upper middle class and identify with and benefit from class privilege.

4) Libertarians often reveal their racism in things they say; not necessarily overtly racist slurs, but little things here and there, such as codewords, that will reveal their obsession with "differences" between races and their denunciation of things that are "politically correct" – in other words, basic politeness for the most part. The vast majority of libertarians happen to be white.

5) Right-wing libertarians are obsessed with conspiracy theories that are completely divorced from reality as well as from a class perspective. These conspiracies are based on jingoism or nationalism and even primitive tribalism and, of course, superstition. In these conspiracies the power of the scheming elites is overwhelming and absolute yet they have been working toward total domination for some time and have yet to accomplish it. In reality, the "takeover" happened a long, long time ago, but that doesn't mean, even though they (the ruling class) are quite powerful, that they can't be overthrown.

6) Of course, virulent anti-communism is a mainstay of right-wing "populists" or libertarians. The writer rants about "dhSTASI." Libertarians constantly scream invective against what they call "collectivism."

7) Conservatives obsess over horrible things and spend an excessive amount of time and energy worrying about child molesters, muggers, burglars, rapists and violent crimes of all types against themselves, their immediate family or their property. They do not AT ALL concern themselves with their conception of a "legitimate" use of massive state terror to subjugate racial minorities and foreigners who "hate us for our freedom."

8) These folks are hyper-individualists and "survivalists." The writer above signs his name as "LoneWolf." This is a term that signifies a terrorist or resistance fighter who fights alone.

Chapter 10: Ancap/Right-Wing Libertarian Foolishness: "Free" Market Competition

These right-wing libertarians (I guess they call themselves ancaps these days) are just too much. They are so ignorant and ridiculous. They don't really understand capitalism at all. One of their central tenets is market fundamentalism. They think that the capitalist "free" market should decide everything. This is what Marx talked about when he mentioned in The Communist Manifesto that the bourgeoisie reduces all social interaction into a market transaction. Everything is for sale and nothing is sacred. Part of their "free" market mythology (calling it free makes it sound nice) is that competition among a plethora of small and local businesses for market share always and forever leads to the best outcomes in terms of lower prices, higher quality, and everything else. These maniacs decry the monopolies as "crony" capitalism; as if there were ever any other kind.

This particular belief about competition is what I want to challenge with two brief analogies or parables, but before that I would ask a few simple hypothetical questions: If you owned a steak restaurant, would you really be excited about a rival opening up another steak restaurant right across the street from you? What would you do about it? Would you put on the kid gloves and play nice, or would you fight to win by trying to the best of your ability to eliminate the competition?

I thought of the first example when I was weeding my small herb garden the other day. The reason you remove weeds from a garden is because they compete with your plants for resources such as nutrients and water. I suppose one of these so-called ancaps, if they applied their market logic to their garden, would allow the weeds to stay. Wouldn't want to be crony monopolist gardeners now would we?

The second analogy comes from 1970's slasher horror films. If you've seen these types of films you know that the victims being preyed upon by the psycho killer will often hit or stab the killer, temporarily incapacitating him, but then they just run away. All the while those in the audience are screaming at the screen: Finish him off! We know that the killer, no matter how grievously he appears to have been wounded, will arise once again to continue the pursuit. Why not finish the fucker off for good?

The moral of these stories is this: Cooperation is best, but when you have to compete, then compete to win. The best way to compete is to eliminate the competition entirely. The competition, outside of sports or games among friends, is synonymous with enemy. Don't just wound your enemy. Wipe him out.

Chapter 11: The Gun Debate – Settled . . . (More Insight into the Conservative Mind)

*Below is an interesting exchange I found online. This person, Karl, really slams a conservative-type in a brief sort of gun debate that is really quite revealing of the deeply psychotic mindset of American conservatives. It's also interesting to notice the very common and idiotic talking points that conservatives are trained to use. For one thing, conservatives engage in <u>projection</u> quite a bit. They constantly accuse others of the character flaws that they themselves are famous for. Another thing I've noticed about conservatives is a growing trend toward denying the political nature of any hot-button issue. They will state quite emphatically that so-and-so issue shouldn't be seen through a political spectrum. "This major issue is something that transcends left or right. This is something all Americans can agree on," they will say. Of course, the simple truth is that **everything** is political.*

Karl Hungus: Ugh, I'm so sick of gun apologists just assuming all we need to do is ask innocent people to be superheroes: Give a 60 or a 6 year old a handgun, and they'll just dive through the air pumping bullets into the baddie while doves fly everywhere behind them! This is malarky! The main delusion of pro-gun fetishists is that Chuck Norris and Schwartzeneggar movies are real. You know what REAL men do when a psychopath starts shooting everyone around him? They crap their pants and sob in the fetal position. The drive for survival is WAAAAAAY stronger than the impulse to be an action hero, and in nature, the survival mechanism is to flee and hide if possible, or at least to try and survive the situation by not calling attention to yourself. That's precisely why police and soldiers receive so much special training and spend many, many, many hours rehearsing the use of force so that they can respond when confronted with violence.

Behind every gun nut, there's the NRA whispering that his family is about to get murdered by some swarthy criminal who wants to sell his toaster for crack; haven't you seen those TV shows and action movies? Behind the NRA is a legion of pro-gun lobbyists all paid for by gun manufacturers who want to sell more guns. Why do all of our modern problems always boil down to some rich business asshole's right to sell his product by any means possible?

stabby_kat: What an opinionated borderline bitchy post. Good luck changing anybody's mind arguing like that. Not very many gun owners agree with the NRA's policies, you're just pathetically stereotyping people and making this into a left/right issue, which it isn't. Nobody, liberal or conservative *[Americans ignorantly equate liberals with the left – the author]*, wants or should want idiots like you armed, or anyone who can't even use a gun properly because he's practically brain-dead either for that matter. But in the arms of someone who's trained for situations like that it can be essential in a matter of life or death, and is UNFORTUNATELY the only way to protect yourself in the event that your feel-good safety net methodology of preventing crime 100% of the time with the power of sunny optimism and a skewed view on reality somehow doesn't succeed. You clearly want to be right all the time (which you also clearly can't pull off) more than you want to put the work in to come up with a decent solution to gun related violent crime, so don't you start preaching to me when you're one of the most uninformed people on the subject.

Karl Hungus: Awwwww, did I hurt your widdle gun-fetishist feelings? I didn't say ANYTHING about right versus left. I grew up with guns and shoot just fine. There are a lot of gun owners who aren't gun-cultists who treat weapons like the solution for every problem and immediately screams, "LIBERALS* ARE PERSECUTING MY GUN LOVE!!" any time someone states a fact that doesn't come printed on a bumper sticker from the NRA.

I just don't happen to believe the way you solve a gun problem is by adding more guns. I'm also constantly amused by the gun-fetishists amazingly moronic action movie ideals, which can be summed up like this: "Those weak, idiotic lefties* just got shot by that psycho, if I were there, I would have thrown down some sweet moves and a pithy line or two, and NO ONE would have died because people like me are totally badass!!! Guns don't kill people, guns kill weaklings who aren't the spawn of Charlton Heston!!!!"

And I'm not looking to change any minds. You people are pretty much a cult living in a fantasy land where all the 'truths' are less than 15 words long, and are dictated by other cultists or by completely amoral lobbyists who know they can count on you delusional idiots to be unable to tell truth from male-revenge-fantasy and be stupid enough to fall for their utter bullshit and buy more guns and ammo that no one needs. We'd need a huge national effort to deprogram all of you to change your minds, and you'd probably start killing everyone else if we tried. So changing minds is right out. We're stuck with you, and you have to live with everyone* in America who doesn't think the solution to gun violence is turning our schools into "Kindergarten Cop".

But I can still point out that at the end of the day, gun nuts are having their base fears and fantasies manipulated in a cynical ploy to sell more guns and ammo in a saturated market. "LOOK OUT! It's inner-city criminals! No, it's international socialism! It's the liberal* gub'mint come to force you to gay marry and burn a flag!" It's always some American that might just need killing, and the other 7 guns you own just aren't enough!

The most cynical and transparent ploy is the new one: "You need to buy many guns to protect yourself from other gun owning Americans, it's the only way!" They've stoked their sales by stoking your fears about every other person on the planet, now they are telling you that YOU are out to get you. Face it, you're a bunch of gullible suckers and easy marks.

(* everyone who doesn't clean their guns in the nude)

Chapter 12: Far Right Conspiracy Theories – Then and Now

Alex Jones, America's foremost purveyor of right-wing conspiracy theories, is simply repackaging Hitler's sick fantasies and ravings of yesteryear. From Right-Wing Watch:

"He [Alex Jones] said that the federal government is provoking people to the point that there could be a rebellion, in which case the globalists would control that insurgency and turn it into a 'socialist/communist-style revolt.' This revolt would then justify federal government plans to hand over power to the United Nations . . ."

Compare that to an excerpt from Hitler's *Mein Kampf*:

" . . . the Marxist fighting forces, commanded by international and Jewish stock-exchange capital, cannot finally smash the national resistance in Germany without friendly help from outside. For this purpose French armies would first have to invade and overcome the territory of the German REICH until a state of international chaos would set in, and then the country would have to succumb to Bolshevik storm troops in the service of Jewish international finance."[3]

Chapter 13: Alex Jones is a Useful Idiot

Alex Jones is doing serious damage to any hope for a broad-based populist, progressive movement in the United States. It is my feeling that this guy is what might be called in the intelligence industry, an "unwitting asset" or a "useful idiot." He is a typical right-wing libertarian, gun-nut, so-called constitutionalist. If I were a CIA case officer or FBI special agent in charge of handling counterintelligence in the U.S. I would definitely encourage someone like this; at a minimum it would be incredibly easy to ensure that he was well funded while hiding the hand that feeds. It may be that he is being "handled" directly by CIA or some other nefarious government or private intelligence agency, but I figure it is at least as likely that he is doing this on his own.

By the way, for those who don't know, this moron has a radio show with at least two million devoted listeners in the U.S. and has produced right-wing conspiracy theory films and operates a couple of websites where he disseminates his nonsense – and he is a Christian who entertains apocalyptic conspiracy theories invoking supernatural end-time scenarios.

Part of the problem with this guy is that *some* of what he says is true (the most effective disinformation will have grains of truth), but he fails to put all the pieces together and he draws the wrong conclusions because he is, or postures as:

1. A devout pentecostal-type Christian

2. A deeply conservative individual, i.e., nativist, tribalist, nationalist

3. An American patriot

4. A thinly-veiled white supremacist

Alex Jones' purpose seems to be to spread disinformation and to confuse and misdirect rebellious youth away from left-wing ideas, values and a progressive populist movement and instead steer them toward a self-defeating right-wing libertarian, reactionary pseudo-populism.

Sincere leftists cannot turn a blind eye to this guy and simply dismiss him. He's going after the same demographic that we are – disaffected young people. My experience tells me that once young people, especially young men who seem highly susceptible to this right-wing paranoia, are infected by Jones' madness it is incredibly difficult to break the spell. Unfortunately, Jones appears to be well-funded through his endorsements of products like water-filtration systems, the sale of DVD's, t-shirts, etc., and other sources.

We need centralized organization and funding to fight back. If the labor unions in this country could ever be torn away from under the wing of the Democratic party and put that level of organization to work for a real progressive movement, and fund a working class

political party instead of bourgeois Democrats, that would surely
help.

Chapter 14: The Spectacularly Insane World of Right-Wing Conspiracy Theories and Who is Really Behind Them!

A very serious flaw in human nature, as it currently exists, is the strong desire to latch on to an idea or message that seems to justify one's already deeply held convictions, attitudes and values inculcated from birth.

It takes tremendous discipline, or just an incredible lack of thought, to not begin to question at some point the basis of society's rules, expectations and organization.

In the U.S. at least, the ideological posture of the general population seems to tack decidedly to the right. You have a terribly miseducated, brainwashed mass of people raised on the mythology of founding fathers, angels and demons, superheroes and American exceptionalism. This incessant propaganda is encountered at school, in church, at the cinema and on TV through various forms of fictional and supposedly factual news programs and infotainment-style documentaries. The American people are reared to be emotional "believers," not thinkers.

Therefore, having been primed to be reactionary (including so-called liberals or progressives), Americans who do begin to question the status quo go searching online for answers; they can't be bothered with books. They are looking for a quick and seemingly plausible answer to why things are so messed up. They want to know why their job got shipped off to China; why there are brown people with more money than them; why abortion has not been outlawed yet; why Congress never seems to get anything done; why there are more and more openly gay people on television, etc., etc.

At this point, after browsing around online for ten minutes or so, some piece of far right new world order (NWO) propaganda is encountered that seems to explain things based on the mysterious and supernatural framework to which they are already drawn due to their upbringing. The basic framework of the story is always the same. There is a shadowy, diabolical group working behind the scenes to conquer the world. Although some of the individuals involved in the conspiracy may be citizens of the nation, they are actually part of an insidious "Other" – an outside, foreign group (literally or figuratively). They may be Illuminati, aliens (UFO's), the United Nations, Bilderbergers, or the ever-popular Jewish cabal. No matter the name of the group or what it may claim is its purpose, what they really represent and what they are trying to achieve is a twisted right-wing horror-fantasy conception of what was called during the Cold War, the "international communist conspiracy."

As Adolf Hitler lamented most notably, this shadowy group employs a two-pronged strategy in its designs for a global takeover; namely, attacks from within and without a nation. For example, international finance (read: Jews) orchestrate an attack on the financial system while simultaneously stirring up racial, ethnic or class unrest within a nation with the aid of Marxist "traitors" from within. White supremacy and ultra-nationalism are also key elements of the NWO story.

The origins of this right-wing conspiracy go back to the French Revolution at the end of the 18th century. This was a pivotal event that shook the foundations of the European ruling class aristocracy to its core. The overthrowing of the French monarchy was a terrible shock to the nobility throughout Europe and they were thrown into a panic. Hysterical and wild with primal fear, they began looking for answers to explain how this could have happened. Unable to think outside of their own selfish interests and narrow worldview, they had to find a scapegoat. The nobility believed their own bullshit and probably most genuinely thought that their station and their privileges were God-given. How could their loyal subjects take it into their heads to dare oppose them and attempt to usurp their power? To many of us today, the answer is quite obvious and simple – eventually oppression will always breed resistance. However, the nobility, in their hubris, were incapable of coming to this realization; to them, there could be only one answer – the Devil.

Shadowy groups were imagined, working secretly to overthrow the Christian kings of Europe; for to seek to overthrow God's divine order automatically put secular, democratic and freethinking organizations under suspicion. The Illuminati, for instance, probably the most popular villain in the NWO narrative, were a real secret society established in the late 18th century in Bavaria to teach and advocate what were, for the time, fairly progressive ideals; for this crime the group was infiltrated and disbanded by the ruler of Bavaria to stave off opposition to the monarchy and the state religion of Roman Catholicism.

One hundred years later, what will eventually become known as the NWO conspiracy theory gets renewed and strengthened with the publication of *The Protocols of the Elders of Zion*. It was first published in Russia in 1903 and it appeared to be the minutes of a secret meeting of Jews, who having co-opted the Freemasons, were plotting to take over the world. In reality, this document was actually created by the Czar's secret police. It was quickly proven to be a hoax; although, even if the document were real, I wouldn't be too concerned about any group of conspirators stupid enough to take down minutes at such a high-level, secret meeting. Such a bumbling gaggle as this would have absolutely no chance of success in their plot for world domination.[4]

I have my own theory regarding these conspiracy theories, and it is that the conspiracy theories themselves are a conspiracy. Decades before Edward Snowden, there were CIA whistleblowers such as Philip Agee, John Stockton and Victor Marchetti who testified about the CIA's many dirty tricks including "black propaganda," or putting out false stories about the communist enemy. One such technique is called "flipping the script." This is essentially nothing more than accusing the enemy of doing what you yourself are doing; for example: "There is an international communist conspiracy to take over the world!" The reality is, of course, that there is an American capitalist conspiracy to take over the world.

Also, when presidents and other high U.S. officials simply drop the phrase, "new world order," in their speeches and other formal statements I think it's safe to say that this is done intentionally to get people riled up. George H. W. Bush and Henry Kissinger (both heavily involved in intelligence) have used the term. We know that political officials choose their words very carefully and these individuals knew full well the impact those three words would have on the most credulous and reactionary of American citizens.

When the truth is so very obvious, the ruling class and its agents must work overtime to muddle, confuse, and misdirect the attention of the population with false narratives such as the NWO story. The best propaganda usually contains a grain of truth and so intelligence operators can lend some credence to the tale by selectively leaking classified information on its own nefarious covert operations, while simultaneously creating or encouraging, funding and disseminating a narrative that presents these facts out of context and turns reality on its head.

One of the most egregious examples of conspiracy manufacturing and propagation through leaks of classified information is contained in the documentary film, Mirage Men. Deliberately leaking selected bits of classified information, or in CIA jargon, "limited hangouts," about top secret test flights of military aircraft have been provided to groups of UFO enthusiasts and investigators in order to misdirect those most curious about these "strange phenomena" and to camouflage (hide in plain sight) these top secret research and development projects while also spreading fear, confusion and paranoia – helpful tactics in the divide and rule playbook.

Realizing that expanding the reach of the NWO delusion could only help their cause, establishment activists commissioned the production of *The X-Files* TV series. This show served to help popularize and bring to the mainstream what had previously been right-wing fringe ideas about a global conspiracy. A major television production is not a grassroots phenomenon to be sure. For those who will protest that TV shows and films are produced simply to make money I would reply – why not kill two birds with one stone? Why not make profits in the short-term and ensure those profits in the long-term by including propaganda messages that will make it so that the population does not directly challenge the status quo – the capitalist system itself. If you think I am engaging in spreading my own conspiracy theories, then research Operation

<u>Mockingbird</u>. Of course, I am speculating about *The X-Files*, but the show certainly does play on the NWO conspiracy theory and there is a clear precedent for this type of thing with the aforementioned covert operation.

Over the years, innate right-wing paranoia and ignorance among both certain sections of the elites and their most loyal, reactionary supporters has, as indicated earlier, almost certainly given rise to many of these conspiracy theories spontaneously, but I think it is also safe to say that, given the usefulness of the impact of these theories to the ruling class, they have surely done much to encourage the spread of these mistaken ideas. I surmise, by the way, that the further you go up the power hierarchy, those elites toward the very top, the power elite, do not at all believe these theories, unlike their predecessors, the 18th and 19th century aristocracy.

While it is undoubtedly true that, given the example of the current Donald Trump phenomenon, much of the establishment fears the potentially destabilizing influence of the growth of far right-wing populism, as long as the proles are chasing shadows and demons they are not chasing after the one thing that could lead to their liberation – Soviet-style socialism.

Chapter 15: How to Identify a White Supremacist

<u>Tip #1</u>

Go to Google and type in "define white supremacy" and this is the definition that will pop up:

"The belief that white people are superior to those of all other races, especially the black race, and should therefore dominate society."

This definition covers all shades and degrees of racism, if there be such a thing; whether racism is blatantly open or covert or otherwise subdued it stems from a belief in *white supremacy*. So-called liberals or progressives are not immune to feelings of white supremacy; and though it will undoubtedly be shocking to many, black people can also be white supremacists. Oprah Winfrey, for example, is a white supremacist; she clearly believes in the supremacy of the dominant white "culture" that is part of the foundation of the U.S. socio-political (and sociopathic) system. And it isn't just the few black people allowed into the ruling class that are white supremacist; working class blacks in many cases experience self-loathing and a distrust of other black people. One black friend of mine told me a saying that was common in his neighborhood and among his peers: "If it ain't white, it can't be right!" Whether it be a door-to-door salesman, insurance agent or a doctor, there existed the belief that black people were either more likely to be hucksters or else incompetent.

So, how many times have you heard this phrase: "I'm not racist, but . . ." followed by a racist, or rather, white supremacist comment? If you are a white U.S. American you will have heard this phrase many, many times. Whenever you hear this phrase you will now know, if you didn't before, that the speaker is a goddamn racist – without fail. Lesson learned.

<u>**Tip #2**</u>

Part of the current Trumpacolypse phenomenon has been the rise of widespread and open white supremacy throughout the US and Europe. A key component of white supremacist ideology is, of course, antisemitism or what I might prefer to call anti-Jewish bigotry. If you spend any time in the comments section of YouTube and other online news and social media sites (those dealing with politics especially, but not exclusively) you will quickly discover a multitude of racist and bigoted comments. These include statements about Zionists, Jews and globalists. The basic message or theme of these comments is that America is controlled by Jews; for these right-wingers it's always some foreign "other" to blame, and the white man is always the victim. I have even encountered comments accusing Jews of being behind the African slave trade!

Some of these comments will be very explicit and speak of Jews being evil or satanic, while others will be more subtle and use the code words of *Zionists* or *globalists*. At other times you will encounter obsessive diatribes about certain individuals or families (*bloodlines* is another term sometimes used) like Soros or Rothschild; these are also code words that mean Jew. If you engage these white supremacist commenters and call them out, they will often (but not always!) deny they are antisemitic, racist, bigoted or white supremacist, but rest assured, they are repeating age-old right-wing conspiracy theories that go back to Hitler's *Mein Kampf*, the forgery hoax known as the *Protocols of the Learned Elders of Zion* and beyond.

White supremacy must be countered and unmasked wherever it is found!

(Below is an angry comment I received in response to this entirely reasonable, self-evident and cogent short piece on white supremacy. It is followed by my response and by that of my fellow blogger, Caleb Gee.) – Prole Center (PC), the author

Hatuxka: So any reference to anything or anyone being Jewish in any way is a codeword for Jews being evil and satanic? Any criticism of Israel (self-identified as a Jewish State is antisemitic? And both identify a white supremacist? So just shut up, only jewish people can talk about Jews in any way. Only right wingers would make any reference to the powerful Jewish people running media, and supporting Israel (being active powerful zionists). Mentioning Rothschild and Soros, Jews who are powerful and Zionist, identifies a right wing white supremacist. What can anyone say? Thanks for letting us know how easy it is to unfollow this site.

PC: I will answer you in the hope that you are just confused and not really a white supremacist. I never said that one should not criticize Israel or Zionism (support for a Jewish state). The state of Israel deserves plenty of harsh criticism, but that is like singling out the state of Alabama for being reactionary when it is just one small part of the U.S. empire.

Yes, some of the bourgeois ruling class are Jews, but the issue is not their Jewishness. Most of the capitalist class are Christians, some are Muslims, some are black, most are white (in the US) and most are probably secular or atheists. None of that matters. Race, religion and ethnicity are not the problem and they don't explain why the bourgeoisie do what they do – exploit the working class and pursue hegemony across the globe.

The problem is with class identity. The problem is the bourgeoisie and their capitalist imperialist system. The solution is socialism. Workers of the World, Unite! Get it?

And yes, when people repeatedly harp on Soros, Rothschild, Zionism and globalists they are repeating antisemitic themes whether they realize it or not.

Caleb Gee: I am very glad to read this commentary! It's crazy how anytime Israel and Zionism's very real imperialist origins are discussed, there are always some crazies who show up and start trying to veer the conversation into one about how everything since the beginning of time is all one big "Rothschild illuminati" conspiracy. Some of them even go as far as to make the United States and its citizens all seem like innocent victims who are under the control of a centralized "Jewish lobby" that forces the US into wars of empire against the will of the majority, something that clearly isn't the case. Yes, there is most certainly an Israel lobby in the U.S., this cannot be denied. But it is not the driving force behind US aggression and imperialist invasions everywhere across the globe. Rather it is just an extension of it.

Chapter 16: Know Your Enemy / Were the Nazis Socialist?

The horrible myth that Hitler and the Nazis were socialists and fundamentally the same as Marxists persists to this day. The CIA, especially, was instrumental in peddling the fable that Hitler and Stalin represented variants of a similar "totalitarian" or "collectivist" philosophy.

Follow the links below to my blog where you will find several extensive excerpts posted from Adolf Hitler's "Mein Kampf", the fascist bible. You have to know your enemy in order to defeat him. These ideas are still very much alive today, but in many cases have just been repackaged a bit. As you read these passages from "Mein Kampf" see if any of this starts to sound familiar. When you hear people like Alex Jones and others talk about "globalists" and a New World Order or Illuminati conspiracy to take over the world, you will know where these ideas come from and that, like Hitler before them, these fascists use populist language to try to disguise the most reactionary worldview.

"It is said that if you know your enemies and know yourself, you will not be imperiled in a hundred battles; if you do not know your enemies but do know yourself, you will win one and lose one;

if you do not know your enemies nor yourself, you will be imperiled in every single battle." – Sun Tzu

Let's heed the wisdom of Sun Tzu and know our enemies as well as ourselves.

Know Your Enemy: Hitler's First Encounter with Trade Unions and Social Democracy (Socialism)

https://prolecenter.wordpress.com/2015/06/21/know-your-enemy-hitlers-first-encounter-with-trade-unions-and-social-democracy-socialism/

Know Your Enemy: Hitler Declares Marxism a Jewish Doctrine

https://prolecenter.wordpress.com/2015/07/05/know-your-enemy-hitler-declares-marxism-a-jewish-doctrine/

Know Your Enemy: Internationalism and Global Conspiracies for World Domination

https://prolecenter.wordpress.com/2015/07/06/know-your-enemy-internationalism-and-global-conspiracies-for-world-domination/

Chapter 17: Why Real American Leftists Should Not Vote for Bernie Sanders

I'm not "Feeling the Bern!"

Real leftists should not support Bernie Sanders for the simple reason that he is not actually a socialist. When asked about socialism he is very quick and eager to point out that he is no Marxist, but rather a "democratic" socialist. It sounds less threatening, I suppose, to your average ignorant American raised on anti-communist propaganda to put the "democratic" qualifier in there; whatever the hell that means.

Besides making excuses for his cute, watered-down version of socialism, Bernie makes it clear that he does not deign to represent the interests of the working class. Almost without fail he frequently uses the terms "middle class," "working people," or "working families" instead.

Bernie is no internationalist, either. This is a key component of real socialism, by the way. Several times in the most recent Democratic debate he referred to President Bashar al-Assad of Syria as a "terrible dictator." He has also been quick to badmouth President Vladimir Putin, condemning his "invasion" of Ukraine and initially (before later changing course as politicians are wont to do) criticizing Russia's intervention in Syria, saying that "Mr. Putin is going to regret what he is doing."

Sanders has stated that he is attempting to lead a "political revolution," not a social revolution. He does not want to fundamentally reshape American society. He's here to save the capitalist system from itself, kind of like FDR did back in the 30's with the New Deal. In an audience before the DNC in August of last year he made it quite clear that he considered himself to be a Democrat through and through. In his comments he indicated that his campaign would be an effort to bring voters back into the Democratic Party fold who had become disillusioned and disgusted with it over the years. His twofold concern (which does not seem to include actually winning the presidency) can be summed up by <u>these statements from his DNC talk</u>:

"I think you're looking at the candidate who can substantially increase voter turnout all across the country."

"If the question is, 'Can we defeat the Republicans?' I think the answer is that, yes, we can."

Some have reasoned that if, against all odds, Bernie is actually elected President, then he will very likely sell out or otherwise be ineffective. However, the theory goes, this will provide absolute proof to the yearning masses, through painful but necessary experience, that the system is hopelessly rigged against them. This is expected to spur them to action to move the revolution forward. Flawed thinking like this only proves why historians are so helpful to society and especially to progressive social movements. The thing is, we've had this experience before. We don't need to go through this trauma again.

The most recent and obvious example of how the system is rigged happened in the period of 2006 – 2010. In the 2006 congressional elections the Democrats promised that if they got control of Congress and the Senate that they would do all in their power to end the Iraq war. They did nothing. In 2008 Obama campaigned as the peace candidate who would put an end to the wars and close down Guantanamo. He did nothing of the sort.

For two years the Democrats had a large majority control in both houses of congress and they held the presidency. They had the power to do practically anything they wanted, maybe even make amendments to the constitution, but they did absolutely . . . nothing! Let it be clearly understood that Bernie has always caucused with the Democrats, he is running as a Democrat, and he always has been, in essence, a Democrat. The Democratic Party is a key part of the political establishment and they will never, ever lead a revolt or even a significant reform movement against the status quo.

Comrades, do not be tempted to support Bernie Sanders in any way! Don't vote for Bernie! In fact, I urge you not to vote at all!

This originally appeared as an article on Global Research on January 27, 2016. (www.globalresearch.ca)

Chapter 18: Thoughts about the Trump Phenomenon

I wrote this shortly after Trump's election in either November or December of 2016. This was my first initial impression of it.

Here are a few points I've been thinking about recently regarding the Trump phenomenon including a few Trump myths that need to be dispelled.

The first thing that comes to mind is a sense of déjà vu that we've all been through something remarkably similar to this before – like in 2008. Now we get to experience hope and change Republican-style. Eight years ago the liberals were euphoric while conservatives were fuming; now we have the reverse situation.

Myth #1: Trump isn't really Republican

To which I reply: Did he run as a Republican? Yes? Then he's a Republican. That was easy. Let's move on.

Myth #2: Trump is anti-establishment

This shows an incredible degree of political ignorance. In the American mind, there is a "political class" and "media class" and a multitude of other communities, groups, special interests, genders, minorities, etc., etc., that are seen and treated as distinct, apart, and often at odds with one another. One group that is singled out for extraordinary persecution is the lowly businessman. You see, big government, those fat cat politicians and union bosses, enrich themselves at the expense of the humble businessman simply trying to make an honest buck to scrape by while providing for his children (and employees). The reality, of course, is that the big businessman (like Trump) and the big government politicos are old pals – they are even the same people. They are part of the same group, the same ruling class. In a similar way, in medieval times, if you took a superficial look at European feudal society you might conclude that there was an aristocratic class and an ecclesiastical class, when in reality they were part of a single ruling class; according to the feudal law of primogeniture, the first-born son would inherit the entire estate while the second sons would often enter the priesthood.

At any rate, Trump has been involved in politics before. He has funded and lobbied politicians and participated in propaganda and political operations; now he has just decided to become a politician for a short while. He has apparently flirted with the idea of running for president since the 80's. Many capitalists do this and then go back to the so-called private sector; they may go back and forth because it can be boring just doing the same thing all the time. Regardless, the private businessman will engage in political activism through lobbying, running an NGO, and assisting the CIA in their covert operations (including espionage, propaganda, economic sanctions, assassination, coups, etc.) by providing funding, technical expertise and agent cover through their corporations. The point is: There is no wall dividing up the private and public sectors. All those ruling class members are in the same club, they play for the same team and they are cut from the same cloth. Even the playboys and jet-setters are expected to kick in once in a while and assist in ensuring that their class, the ruling class, *remains* the ruling class.

Myth #3: The system works. The people have spoken!

The power elite of the ruling class outflanked a lot of us with this caper. By appointing Trump president they were able to show the world that democracy and pluralism work. They were able to make a liar out of all of us, including Julian Assange of Wikileaks who proclaimed that "Trump would not be allowed to win." I believe it is quite possible the power elite (through the CIA) decided it was wiser to let the under(funded)dog win since over 90% of elections are won by the candidate with the most money. Hillary raised over twice as much money as Trump did. The message is that big money cannot always have its way and the little guy is beginning to assert some control over the government. Just keep voting and everything will be fine. The system works. Our democracy is safe and sound. On the contrary, the vote very likely was rigged in favor of Donald Trump according to investigative journalist Greg Palast and professor Mark Crispin Miller, who has studied voter suppression and election fraud tactics. According to Dr. Miller, when the exit polls differ widely from the election outcome, this is not likely to be evidence of bad polling methods, but rather proof that the vote tallies were tampered with. My own feeling is that when it comes to a question between whether the elites and their agents are mistaken or incompetent or whether they are corrupt and duplicitous, I think that without compelling evidence to the contrary, it is safer to assume the latter possibility.

Unfortunately, in their analyses these two gentlemen seem to lean toward the ridiculous notion that the mean ol' Republicans are stealing elections from the timid and perpetually bullied Democrats. The two parties may represent different factions in the capitalist one-party state, but they certainly seem to collude (especially toward the top) a lot more than they compete. For instance, how often have you heard a politico refer to his or her "friends across the aisle?" When they are no longer in front of the cameras, they go back to being quite chummy.

I speculate that the CIA is deeply embedded within the DNC and GOP and allows the two parties to vie for its affection and may tip the balance for one or the other if it has a clear preference. Actually, we should probably have seen this coming. For one thing, following the pattern of the last few decades, it is the Republican party's turn to represent the capitalist ruling class in government. Also, as indicated earlier, a Trump "win" turned out to be the best mechanism for keeping the masses fired up and most starkly divided. If Hillary had won, then you would have outraged conservatives with a lukewarm, perhaps relatively content batch of liberals and everyone else. Due to the fixed outcome for Trump, again, you have euphoric conservatives and irate liberals; it's a win-win!

Myth #4: The (liberal) media favored Hillary.

The teenage daughter that is the American people succumbed to reverse psychology and ran into the arms of the bad boy Donald Trump. Trump received over $5 billion in free advertising from the MSM during his campaign according to Lee Camp of Redacted Tonight (twice as much as Clinton). Trump got 23x as much coverage as Bernie Sanders, by the way. In fact, if you tally up the value of free advertising Trump received (remembering that there is no such thing as bad publicity – especially when it comes to Trump) the maxim remains true that the candidate with the most money wins!

Myth #5: Trump will end all the wars and imperialist aggression!

I see no evidence for this beyond Trump's rhetoric. The important question to ask is *why* Trump and his supporters are against foreign wars. The why is very, very important in determining how likely it is that the US will turn away from its quest for global domination. The answer to the question why seems to be that the wars are "stupid" or "too expensive." I for one do not find this to be reassuring; this is not a very moral, progressive or principled stance to take. All that is needed is another Gulf of Tonkin or 9/11 type provocation or false flag attack and, well, President Trump's hands will be tied; he will have to act to defend America!

Having dealt with several Trump myths, I would like to make a few more observations. The conflation by the media of the far left with the far right and all manifestations of "extremism" has been with us for a long time, but now Trump has become the "pied piper" for all these folks. The ruling class strategists have painted these contrasting ideologies with the same wide brush. Once it was forbidden to speak of the working class because of the Marxist connotations of the term, but now the media propagandists are happy to talk about a white working class in the context of how reactionary they are claimed to be. Sadly, there is some truth to this because the white working class has been reared to be white supremacist; this is enormously helpful for purposes of divide and rule. The bourgeois ruling class would love to encourage and exacerbate this racial division.

Also, I think there is another dangerous and disturbing possibility that we must consider, and it is that the Trump rapprochement with Russia could be a CIA/ruling class ploy to drive a wedge between Russia and China – that powerful alliance is the greatest threat to their plans for global domination.

Finally, in a bizarre twist, many supposed leftists are proclaiming a victory for the people with this Trumpocalypse. This is a strange and dangerous development and has no basis in reality. I really hope I'm wrong and that Trump stops the wars and defies the ruling class in its quest for world domination, but I'm not at all optimistic about that eventuality. We need to keep asking questions, retain a healthy skepticism, apply a Marxist analysis to events and not get suckered by a massive CIA propaganda/psyop/political operation.

Chapter 19: Making Sense of the Ongoing Trumpacolypse (Or Not)

I wrote this several months in to the Trump presidency.

"Oh, what a tangled web we weave
When first we practise to deceive!"

– from *Marmion* by Sir Walter Scott

The political reality show in the US becomes more and more insane as time goes by. I have some more thoughts to share about what might really be going on, especially as it pertains to what I like to call the Trumpacolypse.

There are several possible scenarios that can overlap:

1 – The US ruling class is bitterly divided between far right business nationalists who backed Trump, and the traditionally dominant business multi-nationalists who backed Hillary and lost.

2 – The US ruling class is NOT divided (or not seriously) and Trump is, despite all the drama, the choice of a clear majority or consensus elite opinion.

3 – Russia is involved at some level in influencing public opinion and may even have worked out a deal with the far right business nationalists.

4 – Trump is a patsy of some kind, set up to fail, in an attempt to draw Russia into a trap and/or to discredit and further marginalize and falsely conflate the far left and far right who flocked to Trump for one reason or another, but resist ruling class efforts to bring them into the moribund political "center." (Yes, some leftists fell for Trump's "anti-establishment" pitch!)

5 – If there is a division among the US ruling classes then it has to do with long-term strategy and tactics vis-à-vis Russia and China.

6 – There could be collusion between the biz nationalists and multi-nationalists, who at this stage of the development of US capitalist imperialism, have largely coalesced into one united ruling class power elite and are playing a twisted game of good cop-bad cop to keep America's enemies off-balance and continually guessing at US intentions (kind of like Nixon's strategy of wishing to appear crazy and unpredictable as a psychological warfare tactic against the communists).

The situation becomes all the more tangled and complicated as it is fluid and dynamic and the capitalist power elite are compelled to change tactics and focus from time to time in response to countermoves by Russia, China, Iran and other international players. The great game has become one enormous complicated and increasingly dangerous clusterfuck.

Contrary to all appearances, I have a nagging suspicion that the US ruling class is not nearly as divided as the rest of the population, and this is by their will and design. If a dominant faction of the ruling class (which crosses party lines) decides that it really wants Trump gone, then he won't finish out the year. That's how you'll really know how much they are against him and how much of this media hoopla is real or just for show.

Without getting too carried away, I think we need to consider all these possibilities and especially those that differ from the prevailing narratives being trotted out. As I said, Trump could be a patsy of some kind, set up to fail, and/or he could be what the CIA call a "dangle" used to lure Putin into a trap. It could very well be a carrot and stick overture toward the Russian opposition (the liberal parties in Russia). This "dangle" attempt could also be used to tear Russia away from China and Iran. It is entirely possible that the Trump campaign met with Russian officials and made some sort of a deal (which they may not intend to keep) to withdraw the sanctions and reduce the military presence on Russia's borders.

It is painfully obvious that the Russian government, as evidenced by RT's coverage of the 2016 presidential election, strongly favored Trump over Hillary. This is the real source of the Russian "active measures" and "meddling in our democracy" rhetoric we are getting from the recent Congressional show hearings. No thinking person really believes that Russia hacked the DNC or the voting machines; far right Republican dirty tricksters or the CIA itself probably did that. To the extent that there might really be infighting going on within the US ruling class, it is probably similar to the Watergate affair during Nixon's tenure – a far right faction breaks the gentleman's rules of fair play, inter-party collaboration and class solidarity, and has to be brought to heel.

One way or another, for whatever nefarious end, Trump was undoubtedly thoroughly vetted. The ruling class conflict may itself be "fake news" or, again, its scope is greatly exaggerated. What I find most difficult to believe is that Trump was elected by "the people." Rather, he was appointed through consensus of the ruling class or one of two (or more) factions won out, but things could have changed between the beginning of Trump's campaign and now; could some of them be having buyer's remorse? Lots of contradictions will certainly abound as the empire goes through prolonged death throes – like an enormous dragon flailing around causing tremendous damage on its way out.

Trump was probably employed to serve multiple purposes. One of these that seems most obvious was that he was put out there as the far right polar opposite of Bernie – to bring the fringes back to the center and back into the two party trap.

It is a terrible mistake of genuine leftists to fall into the other trap set by ruling class operators of singling Trump out for demonization while remaining silent or demurring when it comes to the crimes of Obama, Hillary and the Democrats. Obama prepared the way for Trump – or someone like Trump – regardless of intentions or the presence or absence of insidious machinations. The important thing to remember is that we must not fixate on personalities, but rather the social and economic forces behind them.

Trump is a weapon of mass distraction; he serves as a figurehead, both king and jester, while the real powers behind the throne – the capitalist oligarchs of the military-industrial-complex, big oil, big pharma and all the rest are running the show, as usual.

I think that there are several very important points to take away from this:

1 – NOTHING has fundamentally changed in American politics. These events are not entirely unprecedented.

2 – There is no popular uprising underway that can seriously challenge the system at this point or in the foreseeable future,

unfortunately. The American people are not "waking up." The USRC (US ruling class) is dealing with serious challenges to its empire and its fanatic crusade to conquer the globe, but at least at home they are firmly in the driver's seat and they still enjoy a commanding position on the global stage, although it is in decline.

3 – There is an effort to conflate all non-mainstream "extremist/fringe" views, whether on the far left or far right, together in the same "basket of deplorables" to use Hillary's language. Given the choice, of course, the USRC would much, much prefer to steer the population further rightward despite the risks and special challenges this entails; this will hurt the feelings of some liberal elites, but they'll get over it – they always do.

4 – This Trumpacolypse mania has a lot to do with Russia, there can be no doubt about that. Trump's overtures to Russia I believe are bogus. The USRC has nearly lost its mind with rage and hysteria because Russia (and China) and others are beginning to successfully, at least in part, push back against US imperialism. There may have been a faction of the USRC, the far (alt) right who thought they could or should try to unite all the white people against the brown and yellow commies and muslims, but it appears that Russia is not going to throw its Chinese, Iranian and Syrian allies under the bus (fingers crossed!).

And, finally, if all this sounds way too convoluted, conspiratorial or depressingly cynical regarding our precious "democracy," you should always remember that when it comes to American politics, however cynical you are, you can't possibly be cynical enough!

Chapter 20: A Vote for Bernie or Trump IS a Vote for the Establishment

Late Summer / Early Fall 2016

When reading much of the analysis surrounding both the Trump and Bernie campaigns there seems to be a widespread assumption that somehow the U.S. ruling class is in crisis and losing control of the electoral process. This is a fantasy! If only it were so. There is a very high burden of proof demanded of those who would make this ludicrous claim.

It is important to understand that both Bernie Sanders and Donald Trump are clearly members of the establishment. A vote for either of them is a vote for the establishment. Bernie has been in Congress since 1991 – for the past 25 years. Trump is a billionaire, which makes him, by definition, a bona fide member of the ruling class. His antics are nothing short of bad acting; he even has a page on IMDb. Donald Trump has had cameo roles in several movies and TV shows. He has numerous production credits to his name, not to mention his well-known reality show; now he is putting on an even grander show for the American people.

It is my contention that Bernie and Trump are both agents of the establishment deliberately put out in order to provide what the late, great George Carlin referred to as the illusion of choice. They are there to do a job; each has his own role to play. Bernie is there to round up the progressives who have strayed away and bring them back into the Democratic Party fold. Trump is there to do the same for the right-wing camp in order to woo the Libertarians and populist right back into the arms of the Republican Party.

In U.S. Presidential elections there have always been machinations and manipulations going on behind the scenes. According to the first exposé of the nefarious doings of the CIA, *The Invisible Government*, published in 1964, we learn:

"When the public positions of candidates for President are shaped (or reversed) by secret operations which the voters are not entitled to know about, something has happened to the American system, and something for ill. The Invisible Government [CIA] participated in the presidential campaign of 1960. It was unseen, but there. **It provided a valuable lesson for future presidential campaigns** [emphasis mine]."[5]

Furthermore, all this talk of how Trump is splitting up the Republican Party is nonsense. The supposed shakeup in the Democratic Party is just as illusory. A recent MSN article reveals a poll taken of New York residents where 7 out of 10 voters said they would either definitely or probably vote for their party's nominee no matter who it might be. The poll was conducted only in the state of

New York, but I think I can safely speculate that this sentiment will hold true for the nation as a whole; although, time will tell.[6]

To sum up the situation: The U.S. ruling class is indeed facing challenges and difficulties, but they are far from being "on the ropes." With every challenge comes an opportunity and the elites are being proactive in rolling out their latest vaudeville act, the Bernie and Trump show. Please don't fall for what should be a terribly obvious charade in the 2016 electoral extravaganza. Some of you still have a chance to *not* vote in the primaries. Everyone has the opportunity to do good by *not* voting in the general election in November.

Chapter 21: Old-Fashioned and Misguided Morality

Most people, at least in the US, that I have observed seem to have a moral code that is heavily imbued with religious overtones, even if they aren't regular church-goers or overtly religious at all. I have even met self-described atheists who take great pleasure in bashing religion who nonetheless have their general worldview and thought processes tainted by supernatural or Manichaean thinking; it is a conservative disorder where everything is simplistically defined as either this or that, black or white, good or evil.

According to Elaine Pagels, quoted in <u>Right-Wing Populism</u>:

"Many religious people who no longer believe in Satan, along with countless others who do not identify with any religious tradition, nevertheless are influenced by this cultural legacy whenever they perceive social and political conflict in terms of the forces of good contending against the forces of evil in the world."[7]

Anyone who thinks in this way is going to be very confused and come to incorrect conclusions about structures of power and the systemic nature of the capitalist status quo.

In addition to this, overly sentimental attitudes like "love conquers all" and an absurd commitment to non-violence will never lead one to rebel against, much less have any fighting chance of overthrowing the bourgeoisie. Needless to say, these sappy attitudes have been heavily encouraged by propaganda coming from both the pulpit and television and silver screen.

As John Lennon once said, "You know, I really thought that love would save us all. But now I'm wearing a Chairman Mao badge."[8]

Dare I say it? Perhaps it is not love that will save us, but hate . . . or rather, if you like, love for justice and bitter hatred for injustice, and our enemies who perpetrate it and enable it.

Chapter 22: The Two Bourgeois Factions in America: Conservatives and Conservatives-in-Denial

Let there be no mistaking just what a bourgeois liberal is – and it's important to understand that liberalism is a *bourgeois* ideology. It attempts to put lipstick on that capitalist pig. Liberals believe in what they would call a meritocracy, but there should be clarification as to what exactly they really mean by that term. As my first book (Against the Rich) makes clear, the kind of talent and drive required to get rich involves an ambition that necessitates stepping over and screwing over your fellow man through attitudes and acts of dishonesty, callousness, hubris, elitism, classism (as one must generally begin with some measure of privilege in order to "succeed" in a capitalist society) and all-round inhumanity.

Liberals believe in a meritocracy that revolves around *money*. Again, it is a purely bourgeois capitalist ideology in which money is the great equalizer. To a liberal, a brown person with wealth deserves a seat at the ruling class table – this is what makes them center-right / moderate conservatives. What makes the far right (ultra-conservative Republican types) *worse*, as far as it goes, is that they believe that one must have both wealth, *pedigree* and *whiteness* in order to get a seat at the high table. That is the (small) difference between these two bourgeois ruling class camps.

<u>Addendum</u>:

On a side note, it has occurred to me that far right-wingers also obsess over threats and evils that either do not exist at all or else are grossly exaggerated. They fixate on unreal supernatural threats or the vilest type of criminality like pedophilia which surely exists, but its prevalence is greatly exaggerated in their twisted grand conspiracy theories, as well as distracting from the true reason for injustice; it also reveals their own projected sick fantasies and obsessions. They (the rank-and-file) are easily duped by ruling class propagandists and puppet-masters and distracted from the real evils of this world and the means and methods of defeating it.

Chapter 23: Exploitation (not taxation) of Labor is Theft

Libertarian propaganda purposefully takes attention away from the point of *production*; away from the unequal and exploitative relationship between a worker and his boss; a relationship between a rich person who can start his own business, and someone with little or nothing who has absolutely no choice but to rent out his time and labor to the former. Libertarians much prefer to focus all their attention on the point of *exchange*. They like to make us assume that there is no class division; that everyone is an equal actor or player in the game of getting more; that everyone can equally choose whether to start a business or work for someone else, and to negotiate a wage or salary from a more or less equal position of strength. You only have to think this situation through for half a moment to realize how absurd and childish is the view put forward by right-wing libertarians. This is a pervasive petty bourgeois ideology that is just as much a fantasy as the Easter bunny, or God; but it is an enduring fantasy that benefits the big capitalist ruling class as well – even if most of them don't really believe in it.

A common slogan put out by libertarians, or anarcho-capitalists (ancaps), as they seem to be calling themselves these days (in order to sound more hip to new generations of dupes), is that: Taxation is theft!

Well, taxation is not actually theft, at least not the kind of taxation these types are concerned with. They are not concerned about the working class being exploited by private businessmen extracting the surplus value of their labor, and then being taxed by the government owned (or influenced by, in the case of the petty bourgeoisie, who have more pull in this system than they pretend otherwise) by those same businessmen. The libertarians use this grain of truth, but twisted around, to enlist mass support to further their cause of making more profits and paying less of it in taxes to the state in order to maintain this unjust system.

Taxation is a line item on a profit and loss statement. It is simply a cost of doing business that every single capitalist system MUST endure in order to fund the repressive apparatus of the state. This can be a fairly significant cost for the upper-middle-class petty bourgeois businessman, and so he naturally wants to push this burden on to others, but in a capitalist system shit flows downhill, and that is why the tax burden can be comparably much smaller and even non-existent for the big bourgeois billionaire businessmen (say that 3 times fast!) So, again, we see who really benefits from this false propaganda narrative.

All this seems pretty obvious to thinking people. You don't even have to be a socialist to see right through this libertarian nonsense, but lots of young, dumb dupes seem to be falling for this caper. It needs to be countered at every opportunity.

Chapter 24: The Ruling Bourgeois Political Party of the United States

As I and others have said many, many times before there is only one ruling political party in the United States. It is a bourgeois capitalist party with two closely aligned factions. Any disagreement that may occasionally arise between these factions has more to do with strategy and tactics, and choice or priority of targets of imperialist aggression than anything else. The two factions have historically, to some degree, also broken down along industrial lines – oil and gas, banking, real estate tend to swing Republican; technology, internet, and "non-profits" swing toward the Democrats.

Some far right elements have at times infiltrated the Republicans, while a genuine progressive, socialist left has had virtually no success infiltrating or influencing the Democrats; the closest they came was during FDR's tenure and the Civil Rights Movement of the 60's, but the "New Left" in the latter period was a bogus petty bourgeois movement that failed to achieve any lasting reforms of substance to the brutal capitalist and imperialist American system. The truth of the matter is that the Democratic Party protects the ruling class' left flank against a genuine leftist force gaining influence and power, while the Republicans are expected to do the same job on the right flank – keeping out or at least carefully managing the far right. I see the Bernie/Trump phenomenon as in keeping with this political strategy of the one American bourgeois capitalist political party.

One of the major contentions with Russia currently, beyond the fact that it won't bend the knee to U.S. imperialism and stands in its way of total world domination, is the fact that Russia (through RT News and social media) is assisting in the disruption of the delicate balance American elites have hitherto carefully maintained by giving a platform to far right and "far left" voices.

Part Two: Propaganda & Psychological Warfare

Chapter 25: Deconstructing U.S. Propaganda – Case Study: Syria

On January 28th, 2014 the New York Times published an article entitled "Syria Blocks Aid to Besieged City, Dimming Hopes Raised in Peace Talks." This is a perfect example of how U.S. elites, through their media apparatchiks, spread powerful and effective propaganda.

First of all, the front-page article's headline says that Syria "blocks" aid in order for the casual reader to get the gist of the message they're sending. However, for those who read the United States' premier, along with the Wall Street Journal, "paper of record" who need the full story and know how to read between the lines, more of the full details emerge on the inside page where the story continues. The secondary headline on the inside pages seems to contradict the main headline; it says: "*Attempts Fail* in Sending Aid to Syrian City Under Siege" (emphasis mine). The casual reader, which most Americans are (if they aren't completely functionally illiterate), will be led to believe that the Syrian government maliciously "blocked" the humanitarian aid rather than understanding the entire situation which led to the failed attempt to deliver the aid in a war zone.

As you delve into the article you will notice that the Syrian government is constantly referred to as a "regime"; this word has come to acquire a definitely negative connotation. On the other hand, the terrorist insurgents are kindly referred to as "rebels," which elicits a more positive reaction; think of the "Rebel Alliance" from Star Wars, perhaps. If these "rebels" were working contrary to U.S. interests they would be called "insurgents" or some other damning term.

Further careful reading leads one to realize that the Syrian government was perfectly willing to allow civilians to evacuate the besieged city of Homs, but quite understandably are unwilling to supply food and medicine to the foreign insurgency; you don't have to be a military mastermind to realize how foolish it is to give aid and comfort to the enemy. The U.S. State Department spokeswoman is quoted delivering fiery rhetoric to denounce this egregious act by the Syrian authorities who will not allow "women and children" to receive the much-needed aid; "The people are starving," she continues, for maximum emotional impact, forgetting, at least for the moment, that approximately 20% of American children suffer from so-called food insecurity in the U.S.

It is interesting to note such concern for Syrian civilians, whose government U.S. elites seek to overthrow despite President Assad having a majority of popular support. The U.S. ruling class allows a million of its citizens to sleep on the sidewalk and has the largest prison population in the entire world (mostly non-violent offenses), but we are expected to believe that it cares deeply about Syrians half a world away; that overthrowing the Syrian government and installing a pliable client puppet-regime just coincidentally happens to further U.S. economic and geostrategic interests should not arouse any suspicion whatsoever.

The article continues by emphasizing the point that "Assad must go." U.S. elites have not given an inch from their original position when they were fully prepared to attack Syria directly. The U.S. is attempting to accomplish diplomatically what they have heretofore failed to do through funding and supplying extremist, fundamentalist Islamic Jihadists. In an attempt to get readers to sympathize with the terrorists they are presented as the underdogs in this fight. Propaganda, if you haven't figured it out by now, primarily attempts to sway people's emotions in order to change their attitudes, beliefs and actions. The propagandists make reference to "the regime's military *crackdown*" and "the regime launched a series of *blistering* military offensives" and "scorched-earth campaign that left hundreds dead including two *Western reporters*." (emphasis mine). Killing Western reporters? Oh, hell no – now they've gone too far!

Of course, the propagandists behind this article (it probably is a team effort) would be remiss in their duties if they had failed to mention that Hezbollah has entered the fray on the side of the legitimate Syrian government. This piece of information is inserted to throw aside attention to the fact that it is the liver-eating cannibal insurgents that are the real terrorists by referencing Hezbollah, an organization on Washington's officially designated terrorist list because of its continued, and somewhat successful defiance of American empire.

The "democracy promoters" falsely claim that most of the Syrian population is on the side of the so-called rebels since they somehow represent the Sunni majority of the country. President Assad, from the minority Alawite sect, is purportedly representing only this minority religious group. In point of fact, the majority of Syrian civilians, regardless of religious affiliation, support the secular state headed by President Assad and his government that does not *just* represent the Alawites. This attempt at divide and conquer fails when the simple facts are pointed out. The terrorist insurgents, most of whom are foreign mercenaries, *do not* represent a majority of Syrians.

Finally, the photograph included with the article pulls at the heart strings by depicting bedraggled children warming themselves by a barrel-fire on a desolate war-torn street. When you see this type of blatant and clumsy propaganda you should completely reject it and tune it out. In fact, I suggest that you don't read the New York Times or other official organs of the U.S. establishment – unless you enjoy being lied to.

Chapter 26: Google Cultural Institute: Misdirection Propaganda and Controlling the Narrative

"70 years on. Remembering the end of World War II"

May 8, 2015

If you visit Google today, the above message is what you will see below the search bar. This link will take you to the Google Cultural Institute, another bullshit propaganda organ of U.S. elites. This is an attempt to misdirect people away from Victory Day and also to control the narrative of the American version of the history of World War II. The propaganda specialists at the CIA and other affiliated institutions felt that it was too dangerous to do nothing and allow the Russians to promote *their* Victory Day unopposed. And so they set up this little message with a link to a Google Cultural Institute *[sic]* webpage containing vignettes of WW2 artifacts, photos and memorabilia. It dances on the surface of things, as American propaganda generally does in this regard, giving a very superficial accounting of what happened without providing any context or explaining how or why. There is some Russian stuff toward the tail end of the list of exhibits, but again, it's from the American point of view – no mention of Victory Day (VE Day in the UK, but not Victory Day) or of the Great Patriotic War and the fact that the Red Army practically defeated the Nazis all on their own and were responsible for destroying about 90% of the Wehrmacht, the Nazi army.

These guys are so successful because they leave nothing to chance. American society is what I call a *total system* (kind of like totalitarian, but easier to say); it's very carefully managed and they are always on the job making sure that Americans, and others, continue to think and feel the way they want them to.

Chapter 27: In Defense of North Korea (Once Again)

I wrote this as a brief note to RT News, specifically the crew who went to North Korea and produced a documentary called "10 Days in North Korea." The documentary was not nearly as brutal as others I've seen, but it was still a less than flattering depiction of North Korea.

RT, you were not allowed to go everywhere and talk to everyone you wanted to precisely because you are foreign journalists. Are you surprised by this? The CIA has used journalists quite extensively over the years as spies. Maybe the North Koreans know something you seem not to know (or pretend not to know). North Korea is under massive threat from the West, primarily the U.S. That is an indisputable fact. No sane, intelligent or honest person can deny that who has any understanding of the history of the Korean peninsula.

I realize that to us "free" Westerners North Koreans' seemingly slavish worship of the "Marshall" (leader of North Korea, Kim Jong-un) is quite disconcerting, but when you demonize North Korea like you have just done, especially without fully explaining *why* the North Korean people and the state behave the way they do, then you are just reinforcing and providing justification for their apparently correct policy of self-sufficiency, militarization, security and ideological and cultural unity. North Korea has survived outside of the capitalist global order precisely because of strong leadership and discipline. Some aspects of North Korean discipline and unity may go to eccentric or excessive lengths from the point of view of those of us in the West who remain comfortably unburdened by the very real threat of foreign subversion or outright attack; one would think that Russians, on the other hand, or at least those who do not look back on the Soviet Union with complete disdain, might be a little more sympathetic to the plight of North Korea.

I admonish you to please keep in mind that time and effort spent criticizing North Korea is time and effort wasted that could have been more productively spent putting the spotlight on the numerous crimes and evil designs of the U.S. Empire – which is very much to blame for North Korea's (necessary) authoritarianism, isolation and eccentricities.

Chapter 28: Thoughts on Pearl Harbor, Patriotism and the Role of the Media

December 7, 2011

Have you noticed how sappy memorials and remembrances have multiplied tremendously over the years? Apparently, yesterday was the anniversary of the Japanese attack on Pearl Harbor. Due to the proliferation of telescreens in every imaginable public space, I saw a TV news headline that said, "Americans remember Pearl Harbor on this day." Really?

That's Pearl Harbor, in Hawaii, where the United States seized control in a blatant act of imperialism in the 19th century. Once conquered, Hawaii became sacred U.S. soil. The hypocrisy is astounding but no less than expected from the ruling 1% of this country. Of course, you know that the media is owned by the 1% and is their mouthpiece spewing stupid lies and goofy distractions. Once you understand that, the blinders come off and then you can see just how ridiculous and fake the media is. They want us all to believe that we're all one big happy family with mommy and daddy at the top telling us all what to do, feel, and think. We're expected to do all the crappy chores of the household and for our reward we get only the crumbs from their sumptuous feasts. If we dare, like

Oliver Twist, to ask for more, we get a spanking and are sent to our rooms.

Patriotism is a lie! This country belongs to the rich. We are not "all in this together" so long as the few enjoy lavish riches, power and freedom while the rest of us must be their slaves! There is no pride in being an American. This country was founded on slavery, genocide and massive exploitation. Toss any remaining patriotism you may feel in the trash today. Once and for all, forget about this abstract notion of being an "American." Enough is enough.

Chapter 29: Propaganda Terms

Low Income Community

If you live in the US, have you noticed how in political discourse every possible demographic identity, real or imagined, has become its own separate (but equal!) "community"?

Well, I heard a new one recently: *Low Income Community*. When I heard those words spoken by a celebrity on TV plugging some new cause or charity my jaw hit the fucking floor. I didn't know whether to laugh, scream or cry – or all three.

As George Carlin once said, "Smug, greedy, well-fed white people have invented a language to conceal their sins. It's as simple as that."

This is clearly a propaganda term invented to sanitize and compartmentalize poor people into just another political identity or market segment for the purposes of divide and rule.

The Soviet Union Did Not "Collapse"

The type of language we use is very important. People think in language and words can have literal and specific meanings and they can also have nuanced meanings that can affect peoples' thoughts, attitudes, beliefs and emotions.

I would like to suggest that all comrades carefully consider how they speak about the former Soviet Union and how it came to an end. Rather than collapsing, the Soviet Union was *defeated* after enduring many decades of sabotage, economic sanctions, propaganda assaults, diplomatic pressure, two full-scale military invasions and the constant threat of nuclear annihilation. If it could be said that the USSR did in fact, collapse, it sure had a lot of help.

Lame Political Clichés

"Speaking truth to power!"

This is another awful and completely ridiculous slogan for the politically inept and disempowered. This one is in the same vein as the "voices heard" type of obsequious appeal to the master class that will be discussed shortly. Please don't say this and correct those who do by gently informing them that, of course, all the evidence points to the simple fact that those in power know EXACTLY what they are doing and they don't need you to tell them. Simply telling your oppressor and exploiter what bad things they are doing to you is less than worthless when they are fully aware of what they are doing (because they're doing it) and they're not going to stop because you point out the obvious. Have some respect for yourself!

I have heard this cliché way too many times. Could there possibly be a more pathetic, cringing, groveling phrase than: "We want our voices to be heard."?!

What good is that – to have your voice heard – when those in power scoff and laugh at you and don't give one whit about what you have to say; that is, if they really even bother to listen in the first place? Personally, I don't give a shit about my "voice being heard." What I care about is having my will be done. I care about having the policies put in place that I want, and to have the kind of society that I want.

Iron Curtain

Words have power. Many ancient cultures have even ascribed magical properties to certain words and phrases, e.g., names of deities or incantations. The capitalists also realized this and have used their destructive power to dupe and befuddle the masses. The bourgeoisie probably didn't invent propaganda, but they damn sure perfected it – especially the Anglos. In fact, Joseph Goebbels, no slouch in the propaganda department himself, said this about the British ruling class in particular:

"The essential English leadership secret does not depend on particular intelligence. Rather, it depends on a remarkably stupid thick-headedness. The English follow the principle that when one lies, it should be a big lie, and one should stick to it. They keep up their lies, even at the risk of looking ridiculous."[9]

Even the Nazi chief of propaganda was in awe of the relentlessly stubborn Anglo-Saxon brand of propaganda; he would be even more impressed by the American rendition of the modern day.

And so we come to that hateful term – the "Iron Curtain." It has been in steady usage since Winston Churchill's speech at Westminster College in Missouri in 1946. This speech, officially entitled the "Sinews of Peace," according to Soviet historians marks the real beginning of the Cold War. It was in this speech that Churchill officially announced that the WWII Allies were breaking up. He said that "an iron curtain has descended across the Continent." He then proclaimed that "totalitarian systems" or communist "police governments" were in control behind this curtain and that they threatened "Christian civilization." Oh, how scary. But what is really scary is the continued use of this hateful propaganda term 70 years later! I have even witnessed its use by those who attempt to speak, if not favorably, then at least somewhat objectively about the socialist countries during the Cold War (another dubious phrase that should probably be reexamined come to think of it).

So, to use a capitalist expression, the bottom line is this: When you put the word "iron" in front of the word "curtain" a powerful psychological effect is created – a very negative one. DO NOT EVER use this propaganda term and challenge anyone who does.

Chapter 30: Americans are against bullying?

One of the more recent feel-good campaigns, as of this writing, in the U.S. has been the fight against bullying, primarily that which takes place at school. Bullying is a big problem, but it is a problem that cannot be solved due to the prevailing American "culture" of elitism and militarism. Capitalism and a reactionary society in general are the disease and bullying is merely a symptom of that disease. Studies have shown, if you really needed empirical evidence, that the working class are the primary victims of bullying in these societies stratified by class, i.e., capitalist societies.

Proletarian youth are bullied by their bourgeois "betters" and even by fellow proles, but it's also well to point out that bullying isn't just something that happens during adolescence; it is all too common for bullying to take place both before, and especially after adolescence – in the workplace, and in the society at large. However, this would not be obvious to anyone who visited the U.S. Department of Health & Human Services website, StopBullying.gov. Here, the closest reference I could find to any possible class-related cause to bullying was a brief mention of "not being able to afford what other kids consider to be 'cool.'" Race, religion, gayness, and kids with disabilities were singled out as the primary "risk factors" that may lead to bullying. Under a section called *Considerations for Specific Groups* there are listed: *LGBT*

Youth and *Youth with Special Needs*. Class is not mentioned, just as you might expect.

Chapter 31: Superheroes and Princesses: Indoctrinating the Young

There is a disturbing trend in the United States that has been going on for some time now. That is for little boys to play at being superheroes and for little girls to pretend to be princesses. On Halloween night all the freaks will come out and the scariest ones, to me, will not be the ghouls, goblins, ghosts, witches, or vampires, but these goddamn comic book and Disney characters! Sometimes I wonder if I read too much into things, but I really feel that American society is what I like to call a "total system." I would say totalitarian, but that word has way too many syllables and was invented specifically to demonize communism, so I don't like it. Anyway, part of the total system involves the indoctrination of the young. When practically every little girl I know or have heard of is planning on dressing up as Elsa from the latest Disney film, I have to figure this is not an accident. This is no coincidence, it is a conspiracy. I also expect to see a dozen or so pint-sized Captain Americas, probably the most popular comic book character these days, followed by Spiderman, Batman and others.

What could be the reason for large corporations, and therefore the ruling class, to push this nonsense? Why are little boys encouraged to identify with and fetishize superheroes, and the same for little girls and princesses? Quite simply, I believe it has to do with perpetuating primitive traditions of gender roles and expectations. Little boys are expected to be macho and aggressive and potentially grow up to be good little soldiers. Jingoism is obviously a big part of this. For little girls, they are supposed to adhere to a twisted ideal of dainty, pampered and consumerist femininity. I feel like there is also a classist element to the whole princess obsession. The bourgeoisie always envied the nobility and just wanted to take their place. All that "liberty, fraternity and equality" talk was just rhetoric to stir up the masses to do their fighting for them. The divine right of kings mentality is what they're really about. They now want to instill these "values" in children of all social classes. Children must be brought up to know their place and to fill their designated roles.

Chapter 32: Right-Wing Slogans

"A Government big enough to supply everything you need is big enough to take everything you have."

This idiotic slogan is popular on bumper stickers and on conservative websites. It is often attributed to Thomas Jefferson, but is actually a quote of President Gerald Ford taken from an address to a joint session of Congress on August 12th, 1974. I have come up with a counter-slogan for this:

"Businesses big enough to own the government are big enough to take everything you have!"

"Freedom isn't free."

This is a popular conservative slogan, especially among soldiers and their families. Actually, if you look up freedom in the dictionary, one of the primary meanings listed is "the quality or state of being free." Here are some counter-slogans I came up with:

"Freedom IS free – it's right there in the name!"
"Freedom for Whom?!"
"Freedom to do what?!"

"How about Freedom from Exploitation, Manipulation, False Propaganda, Oppression, Alienation, Humiliation, Toxic Food, Price Gouging?!" (etc., etc.)

"The problem with socialism is that sooner or later you run out of other peoples' money."

This is a paraphrase of something Margaret Thatcher used to say. It's completely asinine and misses entirely what socialism is really about and how it works. Conservatives (the far right) are simpletons and I think some of their leaders might actually believe their own rhetoric. They fixate on the instrument of transaction whether it be paper cash fiat money (that can be printed as needed) or even something pretty and shiny (albeit, limited) like gold; as if these things had magical powers in and of themselves. What we, as socialists, want to do is actually seize control of the means of production, e.g., the factories, land, equipment, natural resources, technical know-how, etc. Socialism, unlike capitalism, offers us a much more rational, efficient and humane system for managing scarce resources. Here is my counter-slogan for the aforementioned right-wing gem:

"The problem with capitalism is that it shits where it eats and sooner or later you run out of resources and livable ecology!

Chapter 33: PsyWar Lesson: "Defend our White Women!"

February 7, 2016

Here we go again! History is like watching the same horror movie over and over while cringing and hoping it will somehow turn out differently this time and there will finally be a happy ending to the story – but no, of course, it just doesn't happen.

This is how I have been feeling recently with the lurid tales of refugees harassing, molesting, beating and raping white women. These "animals" are even beating up elderly people on trains and buses if you believe all the hype. Now there is also an unsubstantiated rumor that a 10-year old boy has been raped in Vienna! Forgive me if I find all this to be a bit too convenient, and as I indicated before, I think I've seen this movie already and I know how it ends. I'm particularly upset at how RT and some other supposedly alternative, independent or supposedly "leftish" media are buying into this narrative as well.

These stories are unsubstantiated, exaggerated and (I believe) even fabricated. This is one of the oldest tricks in the book. In the official manual or textbook of how to conduct psychological operations against North American and European white populations, this must be precept number one. Sadly, white (European or those of Euro descent might be a better way to say it) men don't need a lot of encouragement in bringing out the devil in their natures. White supremacy is ingrained into the fabric of their shit-saturated souls. "They're coming for our white women!" has been the rallying cry of white trash since time immemorial.

Chapter 34: Pravda: The Real Truth

Pravda was the official newspaper of the Communist Party of the Soviet Union. It began publication in 1912, but was suppressed by the Tsar, and then by the short-lived bourgeois government, until the Bolsheviks took power during the October Revolution of 1917. Pravda means "truth" in Russian and despite the ravings of bourgeois and imperialist scum, it really was the truth. It reported the news and statements of communist party leaders. It conveyed the party's official position on any given situation or event to all members of the party throughout the Soviet Union.

Bourgeois pundits continue to chuckle with smug satisfaction when accusing Pravda of being Soviet propaganda, which of course it was in the original and untainted sense of the word (political pronouncements and persuasion), but they continue to maintain that it was misinformation. George McGovern, the former CIA analyst who appears fairly regularly on RT, consistently brings up Pravda and mocks it by claiming it was poor propaganda and that, according to him, *everyone* knew it wasn't true. Americans, on the other hand, are in a worse state because they actually believe the false propaganda perpetrated by the media organs of U.S. elites, he goes on to add; that much at least is true. As Grover Furr, an expert on the Soviet Union, recently replied to me, whether or not something is widely believed has no bearing on whether or not it is true, but in his opinion Pravda was widely believed to be telling the truth by party members even toward the end of the USSR in the late 80's and early 90's. In addition, Pravda indeed might have been considered poor propaganda in the sense that it could, according to journalists Andre Vltchek, Gaither Stewart and others, make for incredibly dry reading that apparently did not rouse the public outside of faithful party members.[10]

In the words of Mr. Vltchek:

"East European propaganda was clumsy, compared to elaborate Western one … It was just repeating again and again, mechanically, what was actually the truth. So people got fed up and instead turned towards those colourful and well-packaged lies produced by Western propaganda."[11]

There was, in fact, a big difference between Pravda and the recently dubbed "Pravda of the Potomac" (Washington Post) and other U.S. organs such as the New York Times and Wall Street Journal. Pravda was telling the truth and did not lie through journalistic acts of either commission or omission. Pravda did not package or brand itself in an exciting Western fashion, but it simply told the plain, hard truth. It has been said that truth is stranger than fiction, but if that be the case, then *strange* certainly doesn't seem to be synonymous with either *exciting* or *alluring*.

Chapter 35: What about Whataboutism?

This term, "whataboutism," has been cropping up more and more lately. Apparently, the Americans accused the Soviets of this "propaganda tactic" during the Cold War. Supposedly the Americans would accuse the Soviets of human rights violations (try not to laugh!) and then the Soviets would respond with something like, "And you are lynching black people." The Americans then accused the Soviets of dodging the issue while tacitly admitting guilt of whatever they were accused of. This became known as whataboutism.

Whataboutism is an informal logical fallacy, also known as *tu quoque* (Latin for "you too"). It is also a natural reaction to blatant hypocrisy, but it's not really whataboutism if you deny the accusations and THEN proceed to make your counterargument that the accuser is actually engaging in hypocrisy and/or psychological projection; that your accuser (not you) is guilty of the crimes, or something similar, that they accuse you of committing.

There is another fallacy that exists of drawing a moral equivalency (false equivalency) between the scale, purpose, or circumstances behind such seemingly immoral behavior on the part of individuals, or in this case, state actors. Regarding two ideological and geopolitical competitors we might ask: What are they fighting for? What are their goals? Who is the aggressor and who is the defender? Imperialist or anti-imperialist? Which state is fighting to expand an unjust and evil system (capitalism), and which is fighting for its antithesis, socialism? The answers to these questions make all the difference.

Of course, we are interested in discovering the truth, but we are also interested in understanding *values, motives,* and *ideologies* which inform our political objectives.

Whataboutism is only a logical fallacy if the only goal is to get to the unvarnished truth of an accusation of immoral or criminal activity with no ulterior motives; but political and ideological battles are not fought over discovering the truth; they are fought in order to win greater influence for one's own side. This quote from a Bloomberg article rightly points this out:

"As an appeal to fairness, and to correcting for an opponent's biases, whataboutism is not a distraction tactic but an important weapon against a different propaganda technique, known as framing. In a point-scoring political debate, the side that succeeds in making its description of the situation stick is often the one that wins."[12]

It will probably be virtually impossible to convince the other side, or the other side's supporters, that you are completely innocent of the crimes you are accused of; and you might be foolish to allow your enemy to sustain an attack while you remain on the defensive. In fact, in a CIA manual on propaganda (<u>Psychological Warfare</u> by Paul M. A. Linebarger), the reader is cautioned to stay on the attack and rarely or selectively respond to the enemy's propaganda claims, i.e., engage in counterpropaganda.

When it comes down to it, hysterical claims of "whataboutism" really amount to an effort to stay on the attack, deflect and ridicule criticism or attempts to put a spotlight on one's own glaring hypocrisy. In fact, the United States has historically been keen to beat its opponents to the punch in its propaganda campaigns by framing or controlling the narrative. The US accuses others of the blatant crimes that it commits itself! I have referred to this as psychological projection, but actually I don't think that term fits when it is done consciously and deliberately; when lies like these are told, then the accuser is simply being a clever propagandist.

Chapter 36: Propaganda and Censorship – Theirs and Ours / Case Study: Doctor Zhivago

The American elites never sleep when it comes to their massive propaganda efforts. Recently, I came across a blog article from AbeBooks, an online third-party retailer of out-of-print and rare books. The article was instigated by a client's recent sale of an original, first-edition Russian language copy of *Doctor Zhivago*. This particular copy of the book sold for a whopping $11,000! The reason for the fantastic price was that this edition of *Doctor Zhivago* was published by the CIA specifically as propaganda to be distributed to Soviet citizens abroad as well as smuggled into the Soviet Union itself. The idea was that the book would be read and then passed on to others.

So, why did the CIA think that this particular book would make for such great anti-communist propaganda? For two reasons: Firstly, the subject of the book dealt with such themes as loneliness or alienation within Soviet society, what might be called the *plight of the individual* within said society, and a "corrupted and misdirected revolution" [the October 1917 Russian Revolution].[13] Secondly, no Soviet publisher wanted to publish the book and Boris Pasternak, the author, was booted out of the Soviet Union of Writers for his anti-Soviet work.

As several 1958 CIA memos stated:

"This book has great propaganda value, not only for its intrinsic message and thought-provoking nature, but also for the circumstances of its publication: we have the opportunity to make Soviet citizens wonder what is wrong with their government, when a fine literary work by the man acknowledged to be the greatest living Russian writer is not even available in his own country in his own language for his own people to read."[14]

"Pasternak's humanistic message — that every person is entitled to a private life and deserves respect as a human being, irrespective of the extent of his political loyalty or contribution to the state — poses a fundamental challenge to the Soviet ethic of sacrifice of the individual to the Communist system."[15]

Another CIA memo gave the urgent recommendation that *Dr. Zhivago*:

". . . be published in a maximum number of foreign editions, for maximum free world distribution and acclaim and consideration for such honor as the Nobel prize."[16]

While it may never be proved, I for one feel that it is very, very likely that the CIA requested of the Nobel Prize committee that they award the Nobel for Literature to Pasternak. Should this be a surprise from an organization that awarded Peace Prizes to the likes of nefarious war criminals such as Henry Kissinger and Barack Obama?! It certainly doesn't strain credulity to suppose that the Nobel Prize organization was either penetrated by CIA or else that it (being a Western, bourgeois institution) dutifully sided with its class interests and its class allies.

Before the CIA published two Russian language editions of *Doctor Zhivago*, its very first publication was in Italian by an alleged Italian communist by the name of Giangiacomo Feltrinelli. This wealthy, bourgeois, fake leftist and probable CIA asset defied the wishes of the Soviet and Italian Communist Parties and went ahead with publication of this clearly anti-Soviet book. Feltrinelli received the manuscript from one of his "literature scouts" (a spy) who smuggled it out of Russia and handed it over to him in November 1957. A couple of months later, British intelligence would send over to the CIA rolls of film of the photographed pages of Pasternak's manuscript. Feltrinelli's Italian edition was quickly followed by two CIA Russian language editions. Hundreds of copies were handed out at the Vatican (a perpetually eager co-conspirator with reaction) pavilion at the 1958 Brussels World Fair. Many more copies were distributed the next year at the 1959 World Festival of Youth and

Students for Peace and Friendship. This was only the beginning, as copies of this counterrevolutionary book were smuggled into the USSR for years afterward. As can be clearly seen, very suspicious circumstances surround the various printings and distribution of this book.[17]

The Soviets began to realize their tactical error and tried to change course by offering to publish Pasternak's book with some revisions, but the train had already left the station – it was too late. Pasternak was awarded the Nobel Prize for Literature and the Soviet Union was left holding a bag of shit; they were humiliated and suffered a significant propaganda defeat. Now, this entire cycle of events begs the question, of moral and tactical import: Was it correct for the Soviet Union to censor Pasternak's book?

From a certain standpoint, yes. Pasternak was suspected of being a Western agent, and with very good reason – his book was full of very reactionary ideas and in no way offered appropriate constructive criticism of the Revolution and Soviet society, but was very clearly intended to drag it through the mud. Why should any communist publisher wish to print such garbage? Perhaps the Soviet authorities could have allowed a foreign publisher to print the book and export it to the Soviet Union openly and legally? Maybe they should have, but one has to keep in mind that the Soviet Union was in a constant state of siege. Understanding the near limitless resources of the capitalist West, it might be foolish to simply allow them to flood the Soviet "market" with reactionary literature, i.e., propaganda.

Aside from moral considerations, there are significant risks to engaging in censorship. The various risks can be summed up in one word: *Backfire*, or in intelligence parlance one might say *blowback*. Although they approach it from the standpoint of being unequivocally immoral, Dr. Jansen and Dr. Martin, in their academic paper entitled, "Exposing and Opposing Censorship," give pointers on how to conduct censorship successfully; in other words, how to avoid or mitigate the risk of what they call *backfire*. The techniques to avoid backfire are: 1) Covering up the censorship; 2) Devaluing the target; 3) Reinterpreting the action; 4) Using official channels; and 5) Using intimidation and bribery.[18]

Personally, I don't like the idea of censorship and I would imagine that most people find it to be unsavory; but if you think about it, if you have any strong opinions and beliefs at all you will find it to be irresistible. It may even turn out to be tactically correct in certain political situations (especially if you are serious about winning for your cause); or, to think about it in another way, if not necessarily tactically correct then at least it is a perfectly normal and spontaneous response to negative influences or pressure.

An important thing to keep in mind is that the U.S. ruling class, of course, has and continues to engage in censorship of varying degrees as well as deliberate propaganda and disinformation. Their moral posturing, hopefully, is fooling fewer and fewer people at home and especially abroad, but in order to have a chance at fighting and winning against these bastards the enemies of the U.S. will have to employ every possible means, including perhaps censorship of their own, to defeat them.

For those who are willing to engage in the apparently risky, but possibly rewarding tactic of censorship, here are the five main techniques again with a brief description of what they entail:

1. <u>Covering up the censorship</u> – Censor while pretending with all your might that you are not actually censoring.

2. <u>Devaluing the target</u> – This basically amounts to character assassination, or soft assassination, against a personal target of censorship or those who challenge or otherwise call attention to the censorship.

3. <u>Reinterpreting the action</u> – Trying to convince the population, especially those who cry foul of the attempted censorship, that what you are actually doing may seem like censorship, but it really is not – it is some other entirely legal and legitimate activity.

4. <u>Using official channels</u> – Use official channels or institutions such as legal or legislative bodies to "investigate" the charges of malfeasance in the form of censorship. This is a way of pretending to investigate and punish the corruption

or wrongdoing in a lengthy, bureaucratic process that will stall for time; hopefully most people will forget about the matter entirely and then the problem simply goes away.

5. <u>Using intimidation and bribery</u> – Bribe the subject with legal settlements containing a "gag clause" as is done in the U.S. legal system. Also, the simple threat of firing or lawsuits, including libel suits, might help shut people up.[19]

So, there you have it. Those are the methods you can use to reduce the risk of backfire/blowback when engaging in censorship. The U.S. to this day remains much more proficient in the use of these nefarious techniques than the Soviet Union (an overall force for good) could probably ever hope to be. Some of these shady methods will probably never be acceptable to any truly progressive force seeking to liberate humanity, but if we want to win we had better be prepared to consider employing any and every tactic and means we can to win a better world, and indeed any future at all, for humanity.

Chapter 37: Alexander Solzhenitsyn: A Useful Idiot for the West

He is a bad novelist and a fool. The combination usually makes for great popularity in the US.

– Gore Vidal (Views from a Window)

Alexander Solzhenitsyn was a charlatan and a buffoon of epic proportions. He coined and popularized the emotionally-charged propaganda term *gulag* in his bad work of fiction known as the "The Gulag Archipelago." The book was promoted in the West and taken without question as a true and unbiased account of life in the Soviet penal system. In fact, it was translated by a man named Thomas P. Whitney who had a background in intelligence (what a shocker!). Mr. Whitney was an analyst with the OSS during the second world war. The OSS, or Office of Strategic Services, was the precursor to the CIA.[20]

Solzhenitsyn supposedly gathered the stories of scores of prisoners in the Soviet labor camps spread throughout the country. By the way, the term gulag is nothing more than an acronym taken from "Main Camp Administration;" a shortened form of the full name of the penal system which was called "Main Administration of Corrective Labor Camps and Labor Settlements." The sound of hard consonants must evoke some kind of emotional response that is decidedly negative. Gulag sure sounds a lot more menacing than "Main Camp Administration."[21]

Solzhenitsyn was picked up by state security while he was an officer in the Red Army during WWII, or the Great Patriotic War, as it is still known in Russia. His correspondence, primarily that between him and his close friend, Nikolai Vitkevich, was intercepted. In their letters they spoke of "Resolution No. 1" which was their plan for a "war after the war" in which they would right the so-called wrongs of Stalinism. They mocked Stalin as a "big shot" and as "the moustachioed one." As the Soviet Union was under massive attack by the Nazi army and fighting for its very survival, the Soviet leadership could not be expected to have a sense of humor about this sort of thing. Solzhenitsyn was arrested and charged with anti-Soviet propaganda and founding a hostile organization. The traitor could have faced the death penalty for his crimes, but instead received a sentence of 8 years in the labor camps.[22]

The type of people who were prisoners in this "gulag archipelago" was truly shocking according to the narration from a documentary called, erroneously, *Great Hearts of Courage*, about Solzhenitsyn's sorry life:

"Doctors, lawyers, teachers, priests, scientists, professional people of all kinds – anyone with the courage or indiscretion to speak the truth." *[In other words, bourgeois scum of all kinds.]*[23]

After Solzhenitsyn lied in order to pass himself off as a nuclear scientist, he was moved to a much cozier prison for scientists to work on the nuclear project. While here, Solzhenitsyn began to transform. In his own words:

"I began to move ever so slowly toward a position of an idealist *[sic]*, supporting the primacy of the spiritual over the material and, secondly, patriotic and religious. In other words, I began to return slowly and gradually to all my former childhood views."[24]

Solzhenitsyn was not the first, nor will he be the last, person to find religion in prison. In other words, he began to return to his previous reactionary and conservative upbringing. He returned to his "childhood views." Also, while in prison Solzhenitsyn reportedly "memorized hundreds and hundreds of pages of text" – the stories of his fellow prisoners; their tales of suffering. One might conjecture whether these stories were truly memorized or invented.

Solzhenitsyn goes further in his nonsense:

"Freedom is not to grab and take as much as possible from neighbors or from somebody else. Feelings have been given us for freedom, but God gave us freedom of choice *[sic]*. Before my exile I wrote that freedom consists of being able to act and to think independently of external pressures and external enemies. That is freedom. In the Gospel it says: 'Understand truth and truth will make you free.' This is fascinating."[25]

For Solzhenitsyn, freedom came from God. Is it any wonder that he was quickly handed the Nobel Prize by the West and that they broadcast, through Radio Free Europe (a CIA proprietary) excerpts of his crappy book, "The Gulag Archipelago," as well as working overtime to smuggle copies of the same into the USSR and eastern Europe?

Furthermore, is it just a coincidence that his quote above about "the truth will make you free" mirrors quite closely the biblical passage engraved in the CIA lobby: "And ye shall know the truth, and the truth shall set you free?" I wonder.

Solzhenitsyn defected to the West and settled in Vermont for a time. He was a staunch supporter of U.S. imperialism, urging at one point for the U.S. to return to Vietnam and finish the job on the commies there. In time, Solzhenitsyn began to pine away for the glory days of the Tsar and his anti-Semitism became increasingly apparent to the point where even his previous imperialist backers had to abandon him. The only people who seem to invoke his name these days are nutbags from the far right like Alex Jones.[26]

Solzhenitsyn was an anti-communist, reactionary buffoon and the world is well rid of him.

Chapter 38: Noam Chomsky is a Charlatan

I've been meaning to address this directly for some time now. Too many people admire this guy and hang on his every word. Noam Chomsky is not really a true Leftist. To my knowledge he has never had a kind word to say about the Soviet Union or any of the socialist countries of past or present, with Cuba at times being a curious exception. Also, although he is great at revealing and analyzing the crimes of the Empire, he has no helpful advice on how to organize an effective resistance. In 2008 he actually urged people to vote for Obama! In 2012 he publicly endorsed the Green Party candidate for president of the U.S.; some might consider this a step in the right direction, but it was a strategically foolish and morally reprehensible move. The Green Party candidate, Jill Stein, didn't have a prayer and everybody knew it; such a "protest vote" can only serve to reinforce the notion of the unpopularity and weakness of left-wing ideas (or in this case, center-left at best).

When it comes to folks like Noam Chomsky, the Empire can tolerate their criticism all day long, especially so long as these voices are a tiny minority of opinion, but they come after you when you begin to organize an effective force against them. Maybe Chomsky knows this and is playing it safe, but it would be better if he were to not muddle and confuse people with his terrible and often vague advice on political organization and activism. His politics are aligned towards anarchism or libertarian socialism, which pretty much tells you all you need to know. However, if you try to ask him directly to define his political views he will equivocate. He's pretty confusing because he will quote Marx in one breath and then talk about anarcho-syndicalism in the next.

Chomsky is a naive ultra-left at best and an asset of imperialism although perhaps, *perhaps*, an unwitting one at worst. His job really seems to be to assist in hindering any coherent and effective political organization. If you need to learn more about U.S. imperialism and its propaganda and repressive functions at home and abroad, by all means, Chomsky is a great resource, but please do not look to him for ideological or political education. Do not look to him for leadership in the class struggle.

For more details and information on why Chomsky and his pseudo-left ilk are a hindrance to any kind of meaningful change in the status quo, much less a revolution, consult Stephan Gowans' blog article: The Revolution Will Not Be Televised . . . Nor Will It Be Brought To You By Russell Brand, Oliver Stone or Noam Chomsky[27]

Chapter 39: Thanks Hollywood, for Teaching Us about Revolution!

One pervasive theme in entertainment propaganda is what I like to call "the revolution corrupted." The most recent and prominent example of this theme is contained within the film, *The Hunger Games: Mockingjay Part 2*.

The story takes place in a dystopian future society that seems all too familiar. An all-powerful dictator in his opulent "Capitol" rules over and exploits a multiplicity of "districts" on the periphery. Not only must the downtrodden denizens of these districts slave away to provide massive wealth for the Capitol citizens, but they are also required to send one of their children each year to participate in extravagantly sadistic gladiatorial games where they fight each other to the death.

The series of films, and the books they are based on, are wildly popular and serve two primary purposes - not just economic benefits - although *The Hunger Games* franchise has certainly raked in millions of dollars. The other equally important function of this enterprise is to ensure that there is a compliant, complacent and docile populace that will never even dare to attempt a rebellion like that depicted in the movie. This propaganda campaign (funded by the proles themselves!) will ensure that those profits continue to roll in long into the future. It's a win-win situation, as your standard bourgeois business elite would say!

The propagandists and marketers behind *The Hunger Games* are casting a wide net with a message that can appeal to most everyone, although each political and market segment will interpret it somewhat differently depending on their particular worldview. However, one overriding message is the same for everyone: Revolutions end badly for both sides. Don't try it!

As one journalist noted glumly in a recent article:

"So maybe Hunger Games plays a joke upon the protesters who would pluck political messages from it: it ends by warning them that, nine times out of 10, good people become the bad people that they set out to destroy."[28]

Well, in my humble opinion, that *is* the political message that the ruling class would like for us to take from it, as the aforementioned journalist probably knows very well.

To elaborate on this point, we see that the leader of the uprising is cynically manipulating her followers; in actuality she simply wants to replace the despot with herself. After it's all said and done, the professed lofty ideals were nothing but a ruse to win the support of the people. In the film, we see that the resistance hypocritically uses the same ruthless methods and tactics as does the Capitol under its dictator, President Snow. The rebel leadership also uses propaganda to manipulate the masses under its control.

It is eventually revealed that the resistance is not beneath staging false flag operations that target innocent civilians, including children. Furthermore, and most damning of all the revelations, the audience discovers that the resistance cynically shares the very same goals as the tyranny they are fighting: An unadulterated lust for power.

Besides *The Hunger Games*, other examples of this propaganda theme abound; one such is an Oliver Stone film called *Salvador* (1986).

In this film, an American journalist travels to El Salvador to cover the civil war there between the right-wing junta and a coalition of left-wing forces. The journalist, by all appearances an anti-establishment type, makes contact with both sides in the conflict, but his sympathies lie with the rebel camp; that is, until he witnesses their treatment of prisoners in a key scene from the film.

The leftists have captured some government soldiers after a fierce battle, but before they can take them into custody they find themselves being counterattacked. Outnumbered and outgunned they decide to retreat, but hauling the prisoners along with them will only slow them down. Realizing that, if simply released, the prisoners will just be pressed back into service and thrown against them once again, the rebels decide to shoot them on the spot. The dialogue from this scene makes the propaganda point quite clear:

Richard Boyle: [furious at the sight of how rebels treat their prisoners] Is this your sense of justice?!
Rebel Woman: [In Spanish] It's necessary!
Richard Boyle: [Is pulled away by two rebels] You've become just like them! You've become just like them!
Rebel Youth: This is war! You don't have the stomach for it! Get out!
Richard Boyle: [Turns around one last time] YOU'VE BECOME JUST LIKE THEM![29]

The indoctrination starts at an early age as this anti-revolutionary propaganda message even appears in children's programming. The television series, *Transformers: Prime* (2010 - 2013), is recommended for children as young as seven! The *Transformers* are another mega-blockbuster franchise with movies, cartoons and toys going back to the 80's. In this story you have good alien robots (Autobots) locked in continuous struggle with the bad alien robots (Decepticons). In one episode a background story is recounted about how, back on the robot planet of Cybertron ages ago, a robot named Megatron proposed to lead a violent revolution to remedy the "corruption in high places and inequality among the masses."

However, Optimus Prime, initially a follower of Megatron, persuades the high council of the robot planet to enact reforms to obviate the need for revolution. Injustice is overcome peacefully when the council perceives the innate purity and nobility of Optimus. He is then granted the "mantle of leadership." At this point, Megatron, the revolutionary, "shows his true colors" and storms off vowing to overthrow the council and all who oppose him.

The message is quite clear: Violence is never the answer in achieving social change; better to work within the system peacefully. The revolution will inevitably become corrupted because of its use of violence. It is, or will become, just like the evil it claims to oppose. Of course, we must consider the source of this message. It is cynically propagated by tyrannical elites who, although they pretend otherwise, clearly do not have our best interests in mind, but rather their own.

This first appeared as an article on Russia Insider several years ago, which (if it still exists at this point) has unfortunately become an online bastion of far right insanity. – the author

Chapter 40: The Russians are Coming! The Russians are Coming!

"How do we achieve victory? How do we convince the masses, those billions of people? How do we open their eyes and make them see that the Western regime is dishonest, toxic, poisonous and destructive? Most of humanity is hooked on the Empire's propaganda; that propaganda which is not only spread by mainstream media outlets, but also by pop music, soap operas, social media, advertisement, consumerism, 'fashion trends' and by many other covert means; cultural, religious and media junk that leads to total emotional and intellectual stupor and is administered like some highly addictive narcotic, regularly and persistently."

– Andre Vltchek ("How to Fight Western Propaganda*")*

A true propagandist knows how to create and nurture an enemy. So long as Russia will not bend the knee to the U.S. Empire, it will find itself demonized in all forms of media, but not to worry, I think I have the answer to Mr. Vltchek's question, or at least part of it. What we have to do is expose the ways and means in which the Empire brainwashes the young and continues to manipulate their thoughts, feelings, emotions and opinions long into adulthood. A big part of the problem is that people don't recognize propaganda for what it is; the best propaganda is of course that which is not recognized as such.

A fundamental component of American propaganda is creating and maintaining an enemy. The enemy must be clearly differentiated as an outsider or an "other." Differences such as race, religion, customs, etc., should be emphasized. One such group of people that has incurred the wrath of the U.S. ruling class like no other is Russians – first because the Soviet Union led the world socialist movement which threatened the capitalist system, and now because of the Russian Federation's resistance to U.S. dominance. What gall!

Americans have been conditioned to fear, despise and condescend all things foreign, but nothing so much as Russia and Russians. This has been achieved, and is maintained, in a number of ways. For instance, one simple way to evoke a sense of the exotic or foreign when it comes to Russians is to slip in some Cyrillic alphabet into the titles of movies, novels or other propaganda works. This is done a lot. Furthermore, Russians are perpetually portrayed as being excessively stoic, sinister, duplicitous, oafish and even as cold-blooded monsters.

Remember Ivan Drago from Rocky IV? "I must break you." That was the 80's, but movies released just in the past couple of years continue to feature scary Russian mobsters, oligarchs and politicians – such roles not being mutually exclusive. In The

Amazing Spider-Man 2 there is a maniac stealing an armored car in the opening sequence of the film. He has a barbed wire tattoo on his forehead and it took me a while to realize he was Russian because all he did for five minutes was snarl and roar unintelligibly. Spider-Man finally corners him in an alley, disarming and subduing him and using his web-slinger to pull down his pants revealing polka-dot boxers; for a brief moment you can see a hammer and sickle tattoo on his leg. Nice touch. "This not end, spider!" the Russian thug shouts just before being knocked unconscious in a humorous way.

In The Equalizer with Denzel Washington you have more heavily tattooed and evil Russian mafiosi. By the way, what's with all the facial tattoos?

Even a couple of journalists from the NYT and The Guardian, while making clear in their respective articles that they are no friends of Russia, could not help but find the ubiquitous Russian villain to be nauseatingly cliche.

From The Guardian:

"The way Hollywood sees the world today, nothing could possibly be scarier than crossing swords with the Russians. On film, Russians [sic] gangsters will stop at nothing. They will kill your family, they will kill your girlfriend, they will kill their own employees, they will kill high-ranking members of the New York

Police Department and, if you get them mad enough, they will kill your dog."[30]

And this from the NYT:

"Screenwriters even managed to vilify Russia in 'Gravity,' a movie that features only three on-screen actors and takes place almost entirely in orbit. The space debris that imperils the American astronauts was caused by a Russian missile."[31]

However, according to these journalists, Hollywood is simply catering to consumer demand. This is of course ridiculous. Assuming they believe what they are saying, these guys expect us to consider the pervasiveness of Russian villains, their hideous tattoos, ridiculously exaggerated accents, and screaming, slobbering and murderous ways as merely a coincidence. They are coincidence theorists.

I won't claim that I conducted a completely thorough and exhaustive study, but I very quickly and easily came up with this list of over two dozen films, television (and one video game) where Russians are depicted in a negative light. On the other hand, I had to search far and wide to come up with two Hollywood movies where Russians are portrayed, if not as heroes, then at least with some positive characteristics or a nuanced view. Those films are Eastern

Promises and Predators (2010). And now, a short list of media works featuring those nefarious Russians:

<u>Russian Villains in Entertainment Media</u>

The Avengers

The Americans

A Good Day to Die Hard

Jack Ryan: Shadow Recruit

The Tourist

Tinker Tailor Soldier Spy

Limitless

Jack Reacher

Safe

Salt

Gravity

Iron Man 2

Call of Duty: Modern Warfare 2 (video game)

Red Dawn (1984)

Rocky IV

Air Force One (with Gary Oldman)

Miracle (2004)

Child 44 (with Gary Oldman . . . again)

Rambo III

James Bond movies (going well into the 90's)

John Wick

The Equalizer

The November Man

The Amazing Spider-Man 2

The Assets

A version of this article originally appeared on Russia Insider.

Chapter 41: Anti-Russia/Anti-Soviet Propaganda Abounds – Even in Horror Films!

August 22, 2015

I came across a couple of films recently on Netflix. They caught my eye for two reasons: Because they are horror films (which I quite enjoy) and also because the plot and setting of both films had to do with the former Soviet Union, and by association, especially in the mind of woefully ignorant Americans, Russia at the present time.

The first film, *Entity* (2012), is a ghost story filmed partially from the point of view of a reality show. The story is about the crew of a paranormal investigation TV show that goes to Russia to investigate a remote forest area where dozens of bodies were found, apparently having been executed. Led along by their Russian guide and also by a psychic who is able to communicate with the dead, the crew eventually wind up at an abandoned facility hidden deep within the Siberian forest. They came to Russia to try to make contact with the dead found in the mass grave in the forest, but the real action happens when they get to the deserted building that turns out to be a very haunted research facility / concentration camp where, they begin to discover, the Soviets brought psychics and other paranormally gifted individuals in order to study them and figure out a way to use their powers in the cold war; by means of "remote viewing" or whatnot.

Before I even watched this movie, one thing jumped out at me right away; that was the "N" in *Entity* spelled backwards on the movie poster, apparently in order to make the title of the film somewhat resemble the Russian Cyrillic alphabet. It's not hard to imagine the reason why this is done (and it's done a lot). The reason is quite obviously to communicate a sense of the foreign and play on xenophobic fears. Americans, more than any other group of people, have been conditioned to fear, despise and condescend all things foreign, but nothing so much as Russia and Russians. This particular nationality is perpetually portrayed as either being excessively stoic (devoid of human emotion), sinister, duplicitous, oafish and even as cold-blooded monsters. Both of the films highlighted here are no exception.

In brief, in *Entity* you have the Siberian forest, a haunted Soviet concentration camp (the concentration camp theme is consistently used to conflate the Soviets and the Nazis) where torture and human experiments take place and a duplicitous Russian fellow. What could go wrong?

Scintilla (2014), renamed *The Hybrid*, takes place in a former Soviet Republic where foreign mercenaries are sent on a secret mission to recover genetic material of an alien-human hybrid. They make their way past sadistic and psychotic Russian militias (there's a civil war going on) to an underground bunker containing the top-secret Soviet-era laboratory where the genetic material can be found. It turns out that Soviet scientists recovered alien DNA from a meteorite and fused it with human DNA to attempt to create (what else?) a hybrid race of super-soldiers. In the underground research lab we encounter a bust of Stalin and a portrait of Lenin where he seems to be dressed in drag, or else kitted out like a punk rocker; mockery remains an oft-used and effective propaganda device to denigrate an enemy target. However, the head researcher that the mercenaries encounter in the subterranean realm turns out to be British. Why British?

This film was a Swedish production, but American films especially have always had foreigners (non-Americans) play the part of villains. In this case, when you want a sophisticated, intelligent villain you need an actor who will speak the "Queen's English." For a more grungy and sadistic villain you could use an Arab/Muslim, a Latin American or, of course, a Russian. But, back to the matter at hand – the demonization of communism and Russia more generally – it makes one wonder, if communism was a system that was essentially self-defeating and unequivocally evil, then why do we need to be constantly reminded of that, and so eagerly encouraged to hate it?

Chapter 42: Entertainment Propaganda: The Anti-Hero and Enemy Point of View in Recent Spy Thrillers

September 4, 2015

The Cold War is back, and it makes for great television! If you like cloak-and-dagger tales with plenty of suspense and intrigue then look no further than *The Americans*, coming up on its fourth season, and *Deutschland 83*, which just wrapped up its first season a few weeks ago. Both shows are set in the 80's and both are absolute propaganda, but then again, as I'm always pointing out, it's ALL propaganda. Propaganda notwithstanding, I can help you to enjoy the thrills of espionage historical fiction and wax nostalgic for the 80's with its new wave music, Walkman's and other delights, and do it responsibly (without falling for the insidious messages contained therein).

I felt pretty sure that I had accurately identified the propaganda points made in these shows, but just to be sure I decided to check out the blog of the *International Spy Museum;* this "museum," located in downtown Washington, D.C., is a clumsy attempt to whitewash the CIA's image among the American public, primarily I would assume, teenage and young adult males. Concerning the hit FX channel show, *The Americans*, a blog entry had this to say:

". . . *The Americans* continues to intrigue and resonate with audiences because it remains stemmed in real events. The Soviet KGB really did run this sort of operation and the Russian SVR continues to do so, as we were reminded in June 2010 with the arrest of the ten Russian illegals."

"There is another aspect of the show that rings true: Phillip has started to go native. He observes that everything seems 'brighter' here in the United States, and he openly toys with the idea of defecting to the United States. This is a real problem that the illegals program faced, at least during the Cold War. Sometimes illegals would find the United States or whatever western country to which they were posted more inviting than the oppressive and drab communist country from whence they came. In fact, the International Spy Museum contains spy gear from one illegal who thought better of his work and defected to Canada in the 1960s."[32]

As I expected, the show's producers, who are former CIA men who made no attempt to hide this fact (another disturbing trend where, increasingly, activities previously engaged in secret, are done openly or only semi-covertly), along with their colleagues who run the "Spy Museum" continue to put forward the same propaganda themes regarding communism, e.g., America is bright, clean and more open and free while communist countries are/were drab, dreary and oppressive. This notion, taken to its conclusion, basically says that given the choice those living under dark and dreary communist oppression would leap at the chance to come to the capitalist utopia – the "shining city on the hill." And not only citizens of communist countries, but practically all foreigners would gladly cut off their right arm to live in this paradise of freedom, democracy and lots of stuff!

Another upsetting aspect of these historical fiction shows is that most Americans will interpret them as more or less historical *fact*! While at least realizing (hopefully) that the show itself is fictional, many – if not most – will believe that the gist of the story is nevertheless, "pretty much how it happened . . . or *could* have happened."

But, some will wonder, how can these shows be considered anti-communist propaganda when the protagonists of both series are communists, and communist spies at that?! This is precisely the question and the objection that far-right wing conservatives will proffer. In fact, *The Blaze*, an ultra-conservative, far-right wing blog, had a very negative view of *The Americans;* and, if you really understand just what a true conservative is, there is no mystery as to why they would not "get" this type of propaganda approach. A true conservative sees everything in terms of black and white; they have no understanding of nuance or shades of grey. They don't think it's cute or funny or clever to have godless commies presented as the good guys – it is completely beyond the pale as far as they are concerned. The article on *The Blaze* made this quite clear, as did most of the folks posting in the comments section. There was bafflement, outrage and charges of an ongoing liberal conspiracy to turn America into a socialist country. However, one individual, by his remarks clearly not especially conservative, tried to explain to his fellow readers:

<u>Konjurer</u>: "Common people. Think for yourselves. This is hardly the most controversial show on TV. I've watched all episodes and it rocks! The story is a bit more complex than Reds = Good. That is hardly the case. The KGB are shown to be ruthless and evil. The Russian's *[sic]* have never been portrayed in a positive light on the show…ever!

"On the other hand, the FBI is shown to be the good guys. US society and our economy is also shown to be a good thing. In fact…slight spoiler…this is the fundamental struggle of the spy couple. The husband is realizing that he loves 'arranged' wife and kids. You can see the evolution of his character as someone who likes America…as he states 'the lights are always on and the food is pretty good.' His wife, who is more loyal and brainwashed to socialism, is starting to show cracks in her belief system.

"I think the producers of the show are probably saying these stupid comments *[cheer for the KGB]* to create controversy and get people watching. Give the show a chance…it's some of the best TV in a sea of garbage. Yes, there is some sex* but less that *[sic]* the ABC Family Show called the Secret Life of The American Teenager!"[33]

That was a pretty good explanation of how the show is not at all promoting communism, but on the contrary is actually promoting anti-communism in a somewhat subtle and clever way. However, you will never, ever, ever get a hardcore conservative right-winger to understand that; but the point is, this particular type of propaganda is not meant for them – it is actually meant for liberals. Yes, that's right. Entertainment propaganda of this sort is meant to ensnare those who are feared to be just open-minded enough to possibly be sympathetic to another point of view and potentially attracted to progressive ideas.

You have to speak to your audience in a language that they understand. In storytelling there are two main types of protagonists – there are heroes and there are anti-heroes. Conservatives prefer heroes while anti-heroes appeal more to less conservative, and frankly, more mature and realistic people. The hero is larger than life; he or she may have some slight flaws, but the total package is something akin to a demi-god figure like Hercules. A hero will have a very straightforward purpose and moral code and selflessly fight to the bitter end to achieve the greater good and destroy the bad guys. The anti-hero, on the other hand, is much more ambiguous, flawed and complex. As the website, *Writer's Digest*, explains in the following two passages:

"An anti-hero is a protagonist who is as flawed or more flawed than most characters; he is someone who disturbs the reader with his weaknesses yet is sympathetically portrayed, and who magnifies the frailties of humanity . . . an anti-hero is unorthodox and might flaunt laws or act in ways contrary to society's standards. In fact, and this is important, an anti-hero often reflects society's confusion and ambivalence about morality, and thus he can be used for social or political comment."

". . . this character requires a great deal of nuance to arouse complicated reactions in the reader . . . *[he]* is not simply a bad ass who cannot follow the rules. The reasons for why he acts as he does, along with his self-concept, are important to the story. Another trick to creating a complicated anti-hero is to shape his less-than-moral traits and acts into a profound statement about humanity . . . An anti-hero's actions and ways of thinking demand that the reader think about issues and ask difficult questions."[34]

In *Deutschland 83*, we get a good taste of this confusion in society and moral ambivalence in addition to a European viewpoint. The show was filmed in German and was distributed in the U.S. by the Sundance channel with English subtitles. Like *The Americans*, this show is intended for liberals (who should really be thought of as not leftists, but moderate conservatives/center-right wing) and others with progressive proclivities or who are otherwise not wedded to American jingoism or exceptionalism.

The protagonist of *Deutschland 83* is a young East German border guard recruited as a spy to go to West Germany in order to decipher NATO plans for a potential invasion of the socialist bloc. His cover is to impersonate a West German soldier who is set to become the personal assistant to a West German general. As the story progresses, we come to see the Cold War through the eyes of East Germans and Soviets who feel very threatened by the U.S./NATO, and West Germans who begin to feel like expendable pawns of the Americans. The propaganda is very cleverly interwoven into this drama that shows all kinds of points of view, but the net result is going to reassure loyal Americans and other Westerners and supporters of capitalist imperialism that "our system" is better in terms of morality and efficiency.

One of the more interesting aspects of *Deutschland 83* is that the East German spy, Martin Rauch, is a much less menacing sort of an anti-hero as compared to the KGB spy duo in *The Americans*. It is the type of society that he represents, or is forced to serve, that is presented as menacing while he is a victim who nevertheless begins to realize the "truth" that he is being manipulated by cynical and corrupt leaders more interested in preserving their own privilege rather than serving the common good as they claim. We go on this painful, but enlightening journey of redemption with Agent Rauch.

What we have with these shows is entertainment propaganda designed to appeal to a certain political demographic that is not far-right conservative. You get an EPOV (Enemy Point of View) with an anti-hero as the protagonist. The ruling class uses the powerful propaganda tactic of pretending to give all political perspectives an equal hearing when in actuality there is nothing equal about it. Furthermore, they use a kind of psychological carrot and stick with this particular mode of storytelling in order to drive people away from a historically genuine socialist alternative by reinforcing the rage of ultra-conservatives (the stick) – even when they don't watch the show, but are merely made aware of it – and gently wooing away the liberals and left-leaners from pursuing a genuinely progressive alternative to the status quo (the carrot).

* American conservatives, in puritan fashion, get very upset about eroticism and sex scenes on film, but don't seem to mind violence so much.

Chapter 43: Entertainment Propaganda and Psywar: The X-Files, Season 10 Episode 4 (Home Again)

In a previous chapter I wrote about *The X-Files* as a case study in propaganda, particularly as it pertains to the right-wing populist, new world order conspiracy theory. In the latest season of *The X-Files* you have this ongoing alien/NWO narrative in addition to the ever-popular "Muslims are scary" theme, and what I'm going to briefly discuss here, which is in my opinion an even more sinister and recurrent propaganda or psychological warfare tactic.

In Season 10, Episode 4 of *The X-Files*, Mulder and Scully investigate bizarre and brutal murders of city officials involved in persecuting the homeless. The victims are torn limb from limb by a golem type monster known as "Band-Aid Nose Man." The monster was made from clay by a street artist called the "Trashman" and it somehow comes to life to take revenge against the government officials abusing the homeless. Here is part of an exchange between Agent Scully and the "Trashman":

Trashman: The people on the streets, the homeless, the street people, they ain't got no voice, right? They get treated like trash. I mean actual trash. It's like this: you throw your grande cup, or your pop bottle in the right trash can under the sink, recycle's here, trash there, you tie the little bag, you take it outside, put it in the right dumpsters.

Pat yourself on the head. You're a good person, yeah? You did the right thing, you fought global warming, you love all the little animals. Well Friday come, Wednesday maybe, garbage man takes the trash away it's not your problem anymore. Magic! But it is your problem, because it piles up in the landfill and the plastics leak toxins into the water and the sky, but if you don't see a problem, there's no problem. Right? People treat people like trash . . . I just wanted to scare 'em, scare anyone that took dignity away from the homeless. That's when the violent idea popped in my head. It was just an emotion that ran through my head. An idea is dangerous, even a small one.

<u>Scully</u>: You are responsible. If you made the problem, if it was your idea, then you're responsible. You put it out of sight so it wouldn't be your problem, but you're just as bad as the people that you hate.

This kind of bourgeois moralizing is a very common propaganda theme you find in TV shows and films all the time. It promotes the notion that the victim has no right to fight back against his oppressor; if he does so he will become "just as bad" as them. Scully also subtly accuses the "Trashman" of hypocrisy when she says, "You put it out of sight so it wouldn't be your problem . . ." What can one say about such drivel? It is beyond ridiculous, but apparently it is effective in convincing most people to passively accept exploitation and abuse, and resist only through so-called nonviolence and reformism. Don't fall for it!

Chapter 44: The Occult PsyOp

In North America, in the sixties, you had this massive anti-war, civil rights and counterculture movement. This was of course considered to be a threat to the status quo. Various dirty tricks such as COINTELPRO[35] were employed by America's political and secret police force, the FBI, as well as domestic propaganda, psychological warfare and covert operations conducted by the CIA. One of these, it would seem, was the emergence of the occult as a new pop culture phenomenon and big money-maker; another one of those win-win scenarios for the capitalist ruling class. The occult was a big hit with the kids. In addition to making lots of money, it served three important functions: it distracted and diverted dissatisfied young folks away from communism while also very conveniently pissing off their parents and conservatives in general, and definitely dumbed-down the population and made them susceptible to lots of stupid ideas and conspiracies about demonic possession, aliens, etc. A lot of controversy, false stories about Satanic abuse, and right-wing hysteria and backlash resulted.

Here is evidence to show that occult psyop tactics were employed in the UK:

"British military intelligence agents in Northern Ireland used fears about demonic possessions, black masses and witchcraft as part of a psychological war against emerging armed groups in the Troubles in the 1970s, a study says.

"Prof Richard Jenkins, from Sheffield University, spoke to military intelligence officers, including the head of the army's 'black operations' in Northern Ireland, Captain Colin Wallace.

"Wallace told Jenkins that they deliberately stoked up a satanic panic from 1972 to 1974, even placing black candles and upside-down crucifixes in derelict buildings in some of Belfast's war zones.

"Then, army press officers leaked stories to newspapers about black masses and satanic rituals taking place from republican Ardoyne in north Belfast to the loyalist-dominated east of the city."[36]

I assign you, my readers, the following books to read (see below). The first deals with the occult in so-called pop culture and the second gives some background and more historical examples of how the CIA, in particular, infiltrated and manipulated the arts, including music, books and film, to spread propaganda to serve the interests of the capitalist ruling class in the cold war.

Part Three: Espionage, Dirty Tricks and Subversive Operations

Chapter 45: U.S. Imperialists Put Syria in the Crosshairs

September 4, 2013

The U.S. ruling class may have miscalculated this time. They have set their sights on Syria, but there is dissension within their ranks and among the public at large. The NATO alliance as well as individual member states and stalwart allies such as the UK have bowed out and U.S. elites stand alone. Now, in an effort to save face, these same elites feel compelled to take military action which could lead to disaster.

The U.S. congress began by being largely against a military strike on Syria, but unsurprisingly we now see that resolve beginning to weaken as those who wish to maintain their posts and further their careers will follow orders to vote for war. Likewise, the

U.S. public, if history is any indication, will also begin to shift their views as they come under full-scale assault by the mainstream media which of course is also beholden to the ruling class and will faithfully propagandize the population in favor of war. Hopefully, history will take a turn and the propaganda will fall on deaf ears.

Nevertheless, a great victory has already been achieved by the propaganda machine and that is instilling the "indisputable" belief that the Syrian government used chemical weapons, and used them on innocent civilians. The so-called proof of this has in fact been disputed by UN officials, journalists and President Putin of Russia. It is completely illogical to assume (as the West does so eagerly) that President Assad and the Syrian government would choose to use chemical weapons knowing that doing so would provoke U.S. intervention. And why on earth would they stage an attack at the very moment that they allow UN inspectors to enter the country? It strains credulity to imagine that the Syrian government, which has been gaining ground and is apparently winning its war against foreign Islamic fundamentalists and terrorists, would resort to the use of chemical weapons. Again, this would give the U.S. and the West a clear pretext for open intervention. The Syrian government and military have been successfully prosecuting a war for three years despite covert, and then not-so-covert, assistance provided by the CIA and other Western intelligence agencies and special forces. The insurgents have been given funding, training, weapons, diplomatic, logistical and intelligence support by the West, and despite all this the legitimate Syrian government has been winning the war using conventional weaponry.

Let's ask the question: If not the Syrian government, who would then benefit from using chemical weapons? Who might wish to provoke U.S. military intervention in an effort to oust Assad from power and topple the legitimate Syrian government? The answer is abundantly clear. The Al-Qaeda and other jihadist insurgents. It is they who would benefit mightily from such a false flag attack. They, possibly with the help of Western intelligence and/or special forces, are the most logical and likely culprits of any chemical attack. The insurgents have a clear motive. Western elites have a clear motive. If you take a look at a global map you will see how the U.S., with its junior partners of the Western nations and NATO countries has a geostrategic interest in taking out Syria and installing their own puppet regime there. This move will bring them a big step closer to taking out Iran and further encircling Russia and China.

The bottom line is this: the U.S. ruling class is determined to spread the new world order that it announced after the fall of the Soviet Union. This new world order that was announced by George Bush I is nothing more than the absolute dominance of the world by U.S. capitalist elites. Other countries such as Russia and China – powerful competitors to U.S. dominance of the world – must eventually be brought to heel. Any country, such as Syria, that dares to refuse to open up their natural resources, labor, and markets to U.S. and Western investors and corporate titans must be crushed. The Syrian government has had the audacity to declare, and put into practice, a general policy of using Syrian natural resources for the benefit of the Syrian people and denying the exploitation of its citizens for the profit of Western corporations and elite officers, board members and shareholders who own those corporations. If President Assad would have agreed to "market-based reforms" in Syria, then he would have stood to gain a great deal in increased wealth and stability of rule – he could then feel free to deal with his subjects in whatever harsh way he saw fit; instead he chose to side with the people of Syria and therefore must be punished by the Godfather of the world.

People around the world, and perhaps (hopefully) even in the U.S., are increasingly coming to the realization that nations like Syria are not the enemy. The primary enemy of peace and freedom are the warmongering capitalist elites of the U.S.!

Sources/Further Reading:

http://gowans.wordpress.com/?s=Syria

http://williamblum.org/aer/read/120

Chapter 46: Current CIA Operations in China

It has come to my attention that the CIA has fairly recently begun to shift its focus heavily toward China. Shocking isn't it? One young lady interested in a career at the CIA was told that unless she could already speak Mandarin Chinese and was willing to live in China long-term, they were not at all interested in interviewing her for a job. Shortly after hearing this story, I learned that a friend of mine's cousin (an American) has been living in China for several years now and is married to a member of the Chinese Communist Party.

Based on my extensive studies of the CIA and intelligence tradecraft, these stories got me thinking. I wonder if the CIA is trying to insert sleeper agents[37], including Romeo agents[38], into China in an effort to penetrate the Chinese Communist Party and other Chinese institutions. I can't imagine why on earth the CIA would not attempt to do something like this. China is an officially designated enemy of the US because it is an economic and ideological competitor of the US; and it stands in the way of US conquest of the entire planet.

Chapter 47: Socialism Betrayed: Behind the Collapse of the Soviet Union

This book, Socialism Betrayed: Behind the Collapse of the Soviet Union, is a must read for every socialist! The authors, Thomas Kenny and Roger Keeran, explain the internal and external pressures that caused the so-called collapse of the Soviet Union. After enduring relentless imperialist invasions, sabotage, boycott and psychological warfare, the USSR finally succumbed when the growing black market within its borders created a new petty bourgeois class that backed Gorbachev's "reforms" from the top.

Also, while not revealed in the book, it appears that Alexander Yakovlev, Gorbachev's chief advisor on glasnost and perestroika, was very likely a CIA penetration agent – an agent of influence. He could have been either a witting or unwitting asset of U.S. intelligence.

In the book, in the epilogue, the authors downplay a bit the effect of the CIA on the USSR's "collapse," but mention that their conclusions might be quite different if it were proven that either Gorbachev or Yakovlev were CIA agents. Well, I think we have evidence to strongly suggest that Yakovlev was indeed a CIA asset. It comes from remarks made by Former Deputy Secretary of State Richard Armitage during a Congressional hearing in 2007. The guy who dropped dime on Valerie Plame has now also done the same for

Yakovlev. The transcript of the hearing comes from the Harvard Kennedy School website. Here is the link and the piece where Armitage spills the beans while boasting of U.S. success employing "smart power" during the Cold War:

<u>Hearing on U.S. Security Strategy Post-9/11: Testimony before House Committee on Oversight and Government Reform, November 6, 2007</u>[39]

ARMITAGE: Well, indeed. I think we probably didn't get off to the right foot in the Cold War. But, you know, we did apply smart power.

And let me give you an example — I was being facetious about the Chou En-lai French Revolution comment. But one of the advisers to Gorbachev was a fellow by the name of Yakovlev — he's the fellow who came up with the term perestroika.

He actually, back in the bad days of the Cold War, when we were tightly constraining the number of Soviet citizens who might come here, he actually studied at Columbia. And he studied under a professor who taught him about pluralism.
*And Yakovlev went back to the then-Soviet Union with an idea that pluralism could work. And 20 years later, he was the adviser. **So it took a while to realize that investment, but we realized that investment** [emphasis mine].*

Chapter 48: Actually, History IS a Conspiracy: Studies in Intelligence and Covert Operations

"Public opinion polls in many countries today portray the United States as the greatest threat to world peace on the globe . . . Critics of this [U.S. foreign] policy argue that American presidents have pursued their proximate goals, defined in terms of U.S. power, while cloaking them in the language and trappings of universalist desire . . . The conclusions of this inquiry tend to bear out the critics."

– from the Foreword of <u>Safe for Democracy: The Secret Wars of the CIA</u>

If you don't know the history (at least what has been discovered) and the modus operandi of the CIA, FBI and other intelligence or secret police agencies of the U.S., then you have only a partial understanding of what really happened. In fact, you may have a completely inaccurate picture of history and a deeply flawed understanding of how the U.S. empire maintains and seeks to expand its hegemony leading to the ultimate goal of total domination of the planet. You will draw conclusions and form personal opinions based on incomplete or inaccurate information. You might then misinterpret and apply overly harsh criticism of those nations and groups trying to defend themselves from U.S. domination and aggression. Those nations who do successfully fend off the empire are then pilloried by further US propaganda efforts: "Look at that authoritarian regime over there violating human rights and repressing its own people! That's messed up, right?"

The secret to the U.S empire's success thus far lies not only with military might (although that is clearly part of it), but with an unrelenting effort at secret warfare/covert or clandestine operations. The CIA and other U.S. agencies have secretly interfered in the social, economic and political affairs of many other nations – probably most – by trying to influence public opinion through psychological warfare, manipulating elections, bribing military and government officials, funding and training terrorist groups, funding political parties and even labor unions that they can sway to serve U.S. interests, assassination, coups, etc., etc. If you can think of it, they have done it or at least considered it. They tried to figure out a way to kill Castro with exploding seashells!! They infiltrated the inner circle of several superstitious foreign leaders with agents posing as astrologers to give bogus advice. Read the selections below and you will be amazed, entertained, and horrified at the juvenile, but insidious antics of the CIA and other agents of empire; not for the faint of heart!

<u>A Reading List:</u>

<u>Inside the Company: CIA Diary</u> and <u>On the Run</u> by Philip Agee

Start with Agee!

<u>The CIA and the Cult of Intelligence</u> by Victor Marchetti and John D. Marks

Marchetti remained a conservative and loyal American, but lots of good information in here.

<u>Secret Intelligence: The Inside Story of America's Espionage Empire</u> by Ernest Volkman and Blaine Baggett

Some great information, but a bit of a whitewash too.

<u>Portrait of a Cold Warrior: Second Thoughts of a Top CIA Agent</u> by Joseph B. Smith

Again, lots of interesting details, but also a whitewash. This book came out the year after Philip Agee's expose. It was an effort at damage control.

<u>Deadly Deceits: My 25 years in the CIA</u> by Ralph W. McGehee

This is a really good one. Deals a lot with the Vietnam War.

In Search of Enemies: A CIA Story by John Stockwell
CIA misdeeds in Africa.

Mirage Men: An Adventure into Paranoia, Espionage, Psychological Warfare, and UFO's by Mark Pilkington
A fascinating account of how U.S. military intelligence and the NSA conducted counterintelligence operations to fuel UFO hysteria in order to distract and "hide in plain sight" test flights of experimental aircraft and development of new weapons systems. The truth is out there, but sorry folks, there are no aliens to be found – just lots of spooks (spies)!

TASS is authorized to announce . . . by Julian Semyonov
A spy novel from the Soviet Union! Although it is fiction, it is based on true events of covert operations in Africa during the cold war. This story gives a better idea of espionage operations and tradecraft than the fantastical exploits of the James Bond action-hero.

My Silent War: The Autobiography of a Spy by Kim Philby
The memoirs of the highly-placed British master spy who was a deep penetration agent (mole) working for the Soviet Union.

<u>Man Without A Face: The Autobiography of Communism's Greatest Spymaster</u> by Markus Wolf
Memoirs of the head of East Germany's Foreign Intelligence Service.

<u>Spy Handler: Memoir of a KGB Officer</u> by Victor Cherkashin
The KGB officer who recruited and ran the double agents Aldritch Ames of CIA and the FBI's Robert Hanssen.

Chapter 49: Plausible Deniability and Political Assassination

On December 29th, 1170 four knights entered Canterbury Cathedral and murdered the Archbishop of Canterbury Thomas Becket. The knights did not receive explicit orders to assassinate the Archbishop, but were merely in the presence of their king, Henry II, when he cried out in exasperation: "Will no one rid me of this turbulent priest?" or alternatively recorded as "What miserable drones and traitors have I nourished and brought up in my household, who let their lord be treated with such shameful contempt by a low-born cleric?"

That's all it took to initiate the assassination of the thorn in the king's side, Thomas Becket. The king could plausibly deny that he was speaking earnestly or literally. He could reasonably deny that he actually intended for Becket to be killed.

Chapter 50: Psywar Provocation in Alexandria?

June 19, 2017

I'm sure everything the authorities and their MSM mouthpieces said about what happened in Alexandria, Virginia last week is completely accurate. Don't you think so? I mean, what source could be more trustworthy? It's not like this hasn't happened so many times before. We don't get to ask Mr. James T. Hodgkinson what happened so we have to rely on the police, the media and government officials. They would never lie to us, right?

Seriously though, this incident, even if – and I say IF! – it happened exactly as described by the authorities, has tremendous propaganda value for the US ruling class (and not just the Republicans). The left, or at least what passes for a "far left" on the US political spectrum, has been demonized and the American masses are being urged further rightward in their political orientation. Cui bono?

I have a narrative to tell – one that is at least as plausible as the one told by the authorities:

Mr. Hodgkinson was a political activist like many others; passionate, but alienated and tormented for his beliefs. He was put under surveillance by the feds and he was eventually deemed to be a suitable patsy for a covert psywar provocation. It was discovered that he frequented the YMCA every morning, and that it just happened to be next to the ball field where the two political factions of the one-party capitalist imperialist state play their annual charity ballgame. A perfect plan was hatched. One or two snipers were set up on rooftops or other vantage points in the vicinity. The job was to wound a few of the Republican congressmen and any cops who intervened for good measure. Also, of course, the snipers were tasked with shooting Mr. Hodgkinson dead as he entered or exited the YMCA building at his usual 7am appearance there so he couldn't testify against the established narrative after having been set up for the crime. Next, mobilize all media assets to propagate the chosen narrative of a "mentally deranged lone gunman."

Don't believe this could happen? Think again.

Chapter 51: Viva False Flag (in Vegas)

October 3, 2017

Here we go again! I don't want to say too much about this and I don't feel that I need to because all these incidents are the same. There is a lone gunman who dies on the scene – either by his own hand or shot by the police. No investigation to speak of and definitely no trial. Convenient. As I write this, apparently there has been another one of those knife attacks, this time in France. In Europe the terrorists seem to always attack with knives or with vehicles, but in the US of course you have to have lots of guns involved. The "lone shooter" as the media seem to refer to Stephen Paddock (not gunman – the language is important) apparently had about two dozen guns in his hotel room at the Mandalay Bay hotel – overkill, if you pardon the expression.

Also, as an interesting aside, speaking of the media's propaganda role in all this – I kid you not – there was a redaction in a New York Times article published yesterday. I find it interesting that the brother or father of the gunman is always questioned right away and they always seem to say the same thing, which is essentially: *I can't believe he did this. It doesn't make sense.* Mr. Paddock's brother, Eric Paddock, was quoted in this article just yesterday saying that his brother didn't own guns, was not a gun person, had never been in the military, and that he would have been just as shocked and flabbergasted if his brother, the alleged shooter, had killed his kids! This quote has since been removed. Maybe this is a minor thing, but I am always struck by the fact that the alleged gunman never seems to fit the profile of a killer and there were no warning signs whatsoever. This person just suddenly snapped; out of nowhere they just went totally crazy and evil. I'm not buying it and neither should you. We will probably never know exactly what happened – that is the nature of plausible deniability – but one thing is for sure, Stephen Paddock isn't talking. I guess the spooks (covert operators) learned their lesson, after Lee Harvey Oswald, to take out the patsy right away before he can run his mouth at all and challenge their false narrative.

I don't want to make light of this tragic incident by any means, but I very much question the official version, as we all should. Whether you want to reference Operation Gladio, Operation Northwoods, or of course 9/11, there is a *long* history of US and other Western intelligence agencies, primarily the CIA, carrying out these kinds of black ops. As the eminent and prolific political activist and writer Caitlin Johnstone recently wrote online, **it is best to assume that all terrorist attacks are false flags until proven otherwise.**

Part Four: Miscellanea

Chapter 52: Body Language

Guess which one of these guys is more stressed? To find out, I highly recommend the book, What Every BODY is Saying: An Ex-FBI Agent's Guide to Speed-Reading People by Joe Navarro. The author explains that his system has to do with the "limbic" part of the human brain that is more primitive, mammalian and emotional. These limbic responses show up in our body language and are extremely difficult, if not impossible, to control. While the "thinking" part of our more modern brain can scheme and formulate lies, the limbic brain is completely honest and to the astute observer can give us away most every time; this has to do with our ancient survival mechanisms of *freeze, flight, fight* – in that order.

Navarro says in the book that the most "honest" parts of the human body are the feet and legs, followed by the hands, and finally the face. The face comes last because we have all learned to mask our expressions for reasons of social harmony. Under capitalism, for example, it's a really bad idea to sneer at your boss, no matter how much you hate his guts. However, if you observe carefully, fleeting facial expressions can tell you a lot about what a person is really thinking or feeling.

So, in reading others' body language, you have to look for *clusters* of behavior in response to a certain stimuli – such as a question posed or a specific event or situation. It also helps to establish a *baseline* of behavior for your subject. It may be that your particular subject for analysis is just a jittery, nervous person in social settings and will constantly fidget or bounce his knee or whatnot. These signs should not be taken for evidence of stress or deception. (Oh, so perhaps I should have mentioned that, if it weren't already obvious coming from a political blog, our primary reason for studying body language here is to detect deception, but of course that is not the only reason.) Anyway, once you've established your baseline behavior, then you want to look for sudden changes in that normal behavior in response to a stimulus, again, like a question. You want to look for not only a sudden behavior, but also the cessation of one or more nonverbal behaviors.

Now, take a look at the photo above of Mr. Obama and Mr. Putin. I'll start with analyzing the hands, because that is the first thing that jumped out at me. Just from a cursory glance you will see that, actually, their overall posture is very similar. (This is called *mirroring*, but don't worry about that right now.) So, both heads of state have their hands clasped together with the fingers interlocked. This is a sign of tension, stress or concern. Hiding the thumbs is an even further indication of stress or insecurity. You may notice that Obama's thumbs are practically hidden, while Putin's thumbs are clearly visible. Now take a look at their legs. Notice how Obama's legs are kind of drawn in while Putin's legs are splayed out a bit more in a sort of *territorial display*? Finally, observe their faces. Lip tightening or *disappearing lips* are another sign of anxiety, stress or concern. But when the lips have disappeared and the corners of the mouth are turned down in a frown, this is the ultimate sign of stress, anxiety or displeasure. Who's wearing the upside down smile in the photo?

The author of the book stresses that his system is not perfect and that care should be taken when drawing conclusions, especially when it comes to detecting deception, but when it comes to detecting a person's true emotions, it comes pretty close to perfection *if* you know what to look for. My final analysis: both men in the photo are stressed and concerned, but Obama seems to definitely be at an all-time emotional low point. Putin is concerned, but still exhibiting some signs of confidence and dominance.

Chapter 53: Detecting Deception

"People always have been the foolish victims of deception and self-deception in politics, and they always will be until they have learnt to seek out the interests of some class or other behind all moral, religious, political and social phrases, declarations and promises."

– V.I. Lenin

Lenin was right. Basically, if a capitalist or one of his duly *appointed* representative's lips are moving then you can be sure he or she is lying, especially if expounding upon any of the subjects mentioned in the quote. But there is also a more specific and technical way of discovering deception. There is no such thing as a perfect human lie detector, but the ex-spooks who wrote the book, Spy the Lie: Former CIA Officers Teach You How to Detect Deception, believe they can give you a powerful advantage when it comes to rooting out lies. As former employees of the world's most wicked and dangerous intelligence, and primarily covert action, organization they should know a thing or two about deception – how to use it and I suppose how to see through it as well. The authors of this book, as opposed to the ex-FBI agent's "body language" approach outlined in the previous chapter, focus more on verbal "tells" and less on nonverbals.

There are three types of lies: lies of *commission, omission, and convincing statements*. Lies of commission are, of course, when someone says something that is not true, but the key to uncovering deception often lies (no pun intended) in what IS NOT said. Also, liars will very often get defensive when questioned and use what are called convincing statements. These are used to try to convince the interrogator of the subject's unimpeachable integrity; for example, statements like "I swear to God!" or "I've been a party member in good standing for 20 years!" Other related verbal tells of deception are when the subject gets angry or defensive, equivocates or otherwise refuses in one fashion or another to answer a direct question. There are *referral statements* that a damn liar will use to evade a question. For example, how many times have you heard a public official or spokesperson say in response to a question something like, "I'd like to once again refer you to the statement that I (we) made public recently regarding this matter."

Those were some examples of lies of omission and convincing statements, but in order to uncover lies of commission you should keep in mind that most people, except perhaps true sociopaths, are uncomfortable with lying and so when they say something they know is not true, they will lack conviction or tell a long story or otherwise answer in a roundabout way instead of giving a straight answer – even to a yes or no question. For example, Question: "Have you ever set foot on the victim's property before?" Answer: "Uh, well, before this particular incident took place, yes I suppose I have a few times on various occasions." See the problem here? A truthful answer would probably have been something more like, "Yeah, sure, several times."

In addition to analyzing the answers given, or in order to elicit detectable deception behaviors or "tells," it is important to craft proper questions and to make the subject feel comfortable and not as if he is under suspicion. The book goes into the details of how to ask questions properly and even gives a suggested list of questions for different scenarios. You don't always want to ask direct, yes or no type questions. You want to elicit information that will, over time, cause the liar to hang himself so to speak. Also, like the FBI guy's nonverbal method, you need to look for "tells" within a few seconds of the stimulus event or question. You're also looking for clusters of behavior to improve your confidence of correctly identifying deception.

This is great book to get your hands on. I got it used for about a buck or two I think, plus shipping. Get the book (and the FBI book) and share it with your friends and comrades!

Chapter 54: Abraham Lincoln Did Not "Free the Slaves"

It's true. Lincoln did not "free the slaves" as the quaint expression goes. You should, of course, understand that there never has been a "great" American president. In any case, a book called Forced into Glory: Abraham Lincoln's White Dream, written by the executive editor emeritus of Ebony magazine, Lerone Bennett, Jr., refutes the American mythology of Abraham Lincoln the emancipator. It's all useful lies to mollify and bedazzle the patriotic masses. As Bennett says in the book:

"A growing body of evidence suggests that the Emancipation Proclamation was a ploy designed not to emancipate the slaves but to keep as many slaves as possible in slavery until Lincoln could mobilize support for his conservative plan to free Blacks gradually and to ship them out of the country. What Lincoln was trying to do, then, from our standpoint, was to outmaneuver the real emancipators and to contain the emancipation tide, which had reached such a dangerous intensity that it threatened his ability to govern and to run the war machinery."[40]

Now, here are some damning quotes from the "great" man himself:

Lincoln–Douglas debates (1858)

I will say then that I am not, nor ever have been, in favor of bringing about in any way the social and political equality of the white and black races, that I am not, nor ever have been, in favor of making voters or jurors of negroes, nor of qualifying them to hold office, nor to intermarry with white people; and I will say in addition to this that there is a physical difference between the white and black races which I believe will forever forbid the two races living together on terms of social and political equality. And inasmuch as they cannot so live, while they do remain together there must be the position of superior and inferior, and I as much as any other man am in favor of having the superior position assigned to the white race.

Second State of the Union address (1862)

I can not make it better known than it already is that I strongly favor colonization . . . Labor is like any other commodity in the market—increase the demand for it and you increase the price of it. Reduce the supply of black labor by colonizing the black laborer out of the country, and by precisely so much you increase the demand for and wages of white labor.

Emancipation Proclamation (1863)

That on the first day of January, in the year of our Lord one thousand eight hundred and sixty-three, all persons held as slaves within any State or designated part of a State, the people whereof shall then be in rebellion against the United States, shall be then, thenceforward, and forever free; and the Executive Government of the United States, including the military and naval authority thereof, will recognize and maintain the freedom of such persons, and will do no act or acts to repress such persons, or any of them, in any efforts they may make for their actual freedom. **[Notice that this "proclamation" accomplished not a damn thing. You're going to free the slaves outside of your control? Behind enemy lines, deep in enemy territory? How mighty white of you, Mr. Lincoln! It was political posturing – nothing more. – the author]**[41]

Chapter 55: Someone You Know is a Sociopath

Mental health professionals estimate that sociopaths (or psychopaths, if you prefer) make up about 4% of the U.S. population; these are full-blown sociopaths, I take it. I have a hypothesis that sociopathy is a sliding scale and there are many screw-ups "walkin' the streets" as conservatives like to say, that exhibit many of the characteristics of a sociopath. A "true" sociopath has absolutely no conscience whatsoever and cannot feel remorse – not even a little bit. They have no qualms about hurting or manipulating people to get what they want; selfish is not a strong enough word to describe their self-seeking, parasitic behavior.

See the checklist below for recognizing sociopaths, but when in doubt, just assume that anyone from the upper-middle and upper classes are sociopaths. In fact, studies have shown that the CEO of a company, for instance, is at least four times as likely to be a sociopath as the "guy sweeping the floor." The bourgeoisie and the capitalist system are sociopathic and since they are the ruling class, they define the prevailing values (anti-values, I call them) of societies they own and control; therefore, while less prevalent, there will of course appear sociopaths among the working class as well. Be on your guard. In my experience, it seems that North American proles, at least, tend to wear their heart on their sleeve. As an East

German comrade once said: "Americans have a 'confessional' culture." That's a nice way of saying that Americans like to spill their fuckin' guts and tell everyone their business (Facebook comes to mind). You have to be smarter than that. I'm also reminded of the popular film of yesteryear, "The Godfather," where Marlon Brando chastises his eldest son for speaking his mind too freely during a meeting with a potentially rival hood. He says, "Never tell anyone outside the family what you're thinking again." Exercise a little discretion. Don't let these psychos get an edge on you.

Antisocial personality disorder signs and symptoms may include[42]:

- Disregard for right and wrong
- Persistent lying or deceit to exploit others
- Being callous, cynical and disrespectful of others
- Using charm or wit to manipulate others for personal gain or personal pleasure
- Arrogance, a sense of superiority and being extremely opinionated
- Recurring problems with the law, including criminal behavior
- Repeatedly violating the rights of others through intimidation and dishonesty
- Impulsiveness or failure to plan ahead

- Hostility, significant irritability, agitation, aggression or violence

- Lack of empathy for others and lack of remorse about harming others

- Unnecessary risk-taking or dangerous behavior with no regard for the safety of self or others

- Poor or abusive relationships

- Failure to consider the negative consequences of behavior or learn from them

- Being consistently irresponsible and repeatedly failing to fulfill work or financial obligations

Chapter 56: Political Jokes and Parables

<u>Divide & Conquer – Works Every Time!</u>

A CEO, a union worker, and a conservative, non-union worker are sitting at a table. There is a plate with a dozen twinkies on it. The CEO grabs 11 twinkies and turns to the non-union worker and says, "Watch out for that union guy, he is trying to steal your twinkie."

<u>The Camel's Nose in the Tent</u>

As I was listening to a comrade describe his union's dealings with management and the sly ways in which the latter were slowly but surely working to undermine the strength and unity of the union, I thought of the following parable:

One cold night, as an Arab sat in his tent, a camel gently thrust his nose under the flap and looked in. "Master," he said, "let me put my nose in your tent. It's cold and stormy out here." "By all means," said the Arab, "and welcome" as he turned over and went to sleep. A little later the Arab awoke to find that the camel had not only put his nose in the tent but his head and neck also. The camel, who had been turning his head from side to side, said, "I will take but little more room if I place my forelegs within the tent. It is difficult standing out here." "Yes, you may put your forelegs within," said the Arab, moving a little to make room, for the tent was small.

Finally, the camel said, "May I not stand wholly inside? I keep the tent open by standing as I do." "Yes, yes," said the Arab. "Come wholly inside. Perhaps it will be better for both of us." So the camel crowded in. The Arab with difficulty in the crowded quarters again went to sleep. When he woke up the next time, he was outside in the cold and the camel had the tent to himself.

It is wise to resist the very beginnings of evil.

<u>The Boy and the Starfish</u>

A small boy lived by the ocean. He loved the creatures of the sea, especially the starfish, and spent much of his time exploring the seashore. One day he learned there would be a minus tide that would leave the starfish stranded on the sand. The day of the tide he went down to the beach and began picking up stranded starfish and tossing them back into the sea. An elderly man who lived next door came down to the beach to see what he was doing. "I'm saving the starfish," the boy proudly declared. When the neighbor saw all of the stranded starfish, he shook his head and said "I'm sorry to disappoint you, young man, buf if you look down the beach one way, there are stranded starfish as far as the eye can see. And if you look down the beach the other way, it's the same. One little boy like you isn't going to make much of a difference." The boy thought about this for a moment. Then he reached his small hand down to the sand, picked up a starfish, tossed it out into the ocean and said, "I sure made a difference for that one."

Then, turning to face the old man, he kicked him squarely in the nuts. As the old man crumpled into the sand grasping his groin and groaning pitifully, the boy wagged his finger and calmly, but sternly said, "Don't ever again try to deter someone in pursuit of a righteous cause, you cynical old bastard." (The Prole Center addition to the story)

The Angry Teacher (East Germany)[43]

The GDR's (German Democratic Republic) educational system apparently was not perfect:

A high-school teacher asks his class: "Who wrote The Communist Manifesto?"

"Not I, not I, I didn't do it," all the pupils respond quickly.

Aggravated at how little of Marxism-Leninism they know, he tells the story at home to his wife that evening, and she says, "I don't know why you're so upset, maybe it really wasn't any of them."

Now really upset, the teacher storms out of the house and goes down to the neighborhood bar for a drink. He meets a stranger and tells him the story.

"Don't worry," says the stranger, "I'm from the Stasi. Don't worry, we'll get to the bottom of it, we'll find out quickly enough who wrote it!"

The Alcoholic Worker (East Germany)[44]

Apparently, in the estimation of some citizens, the GDR's commitment to egalitarianism went a bit too far:

An alcoholic worker's family goes to the head of the factory where he works and says, "We're worried about our Willie, he spends all the money he gets on drink. Please give him a promotion so he'll have less money and won't drink so much!"

A Terrible Nightmare (Bulgaria)[45]

A woman wakes in the middle of the night and sits up in bed. She leaps out of bed and rushes to look in the medicine cabinet. She runs to the kitchen to open the refrigerator. She turns to the window, opens it, and looks out on the street. Breathing a sigh of relief, she returns to bed.

Wakened by her frantic activity, her husband asks, "What's wrong?"

"I had a dreadful nightmare," she says. "I dreamed that we could once again afford to buy medicine, that the refrigerator was full of food, and that the streets were safe and clean."

"How can that be a nightmare?" her husband asks.

"I thought that communism was back," she says, shaking her head.

Chapter 57: Stories from Communist Countries

East Germany

May 11, 1990

The *Berliner Zeitung* carries a straight-faced account of a meeting of doctors from East and West. Four hundred doctors were invited by a private firm, a bank providing loans to doctors, on a boat trip from Tegel to Wannsee. The West speaker is quoted as telling his East German (woman) counterpart, "Stop acting like an ordinary worker in an ordinary trade, you're not a baker or a shoemaker, you're a professional. For heaven's sake get out of the trade union, you should have a professional association. Stop considering the health insurance program as your partner; start figuring out how to make money out of each injection. Then the new equipment you need will take care of itself."

Classic: in other words, change what's best in the system now.[46]

February 8, 1990

Last night Frances suddenly developed pain in her knee and could hardly walk. We decided to call a doctor; but how? The telephone book has five full pages of different medical facilities: clinics, polyclinics, medical practices, hospitals, emergency services, nurses stations, local health centers, and neighborhood medical offices. If they all exist, the health services must be terrific and/or very bureaucratic. I call the nearest "medical practice" and ask if they make house calls. For what reason, I am asked. I say that we live on the fifth floor and my wife can hardly get from one room to another. The nurse says that we should call the emergency service. I demur, but then call, explain, say that it's not urgent. No matter, we'll be glad to come. When? Within two hours, depending on what other calls we get. I'm astonished, and even more so when, in about an hour, a young doctor with an emergency service shoulder patch and a substantial bag arrives and climbs the four flights of stairs to our apartment. She examines Frances carefully and thoroughly, writes out three prescriptions, and explains their purpose and how to use them. She answers our questions clearly and competently before leaving. Never a question of who we are, where we're from, are we covered, will we pay.

I take the prescriptions to the pharmacy up the street. The pharmacist gets the three medications out of different drawers. As she hands them to me, I am not sure if I have to pay or at least show my passport and identify myself, but she has already turned away to do something else. Hardly a bureaucratic procedure![47]

Soviet Union

I can't imagine why anybody is surprised to hear when I say I miss life in the Soviet Union: what is bad about free healthcare and education, guaranteed employment, guaranteed free housing? No rent or mortgage of any kind, only utilities, but they were subsidized too, so it was really pennies. Now, to be honest, there was a waiting list to get those apartments, so some people got them quicker, some people had to wait for years, it all depended on where you worked. And there were no homeless people, and crime was way lower. As a first grader I was taking the public transportation to go to school, which was about 1 hour away by bus (it was a big city, about the size of Washington DC, we lived on the outskirts, and my school was downtown), and it was fine, all other kids were doing it. Can you even imagine this being done now? I am not saying everything was perfect, but overall, it is a more stable and socially just system, fair to everybody, nobody was left behind. This is what I miss: peace and stability, and not being afraid of the future.

Problem is, nobody believes it, they will say that I am a brainwashed "tovarish" [comrade]. I've tried to argue with Americans about this before, but just gave up now. They just refuse to believe anything that contradicts what CNN has been telling them for all their lives. One lady once told me: "You just don't know what was going on there, because you did not have freedom of speech, but we, Americans, knew everything, because we could read about all of this in our media." I told her "I was right there! I did not need to read about this in the media, I lived that life!" but she still was unconvinced! You will not believe what she said: "Yes, maybe, but we have more stuff!" Seriously, having 50 kinds of cereal available in the store, and walmarts *[sic]* full of plastic junk is more valuable to Americans than a stable and secure life, and social justice for everybody?

Of course, there are people who lived in the Soviet Union who disagree with me, and I talked to them too, but I find their reasons just as silly. I heard one Russian lady whose argument was that Stalin killed "30, no 40 million people." First of all it's not true (I don't in any way defend Stalin, but I do think that lying and exaggerating about him is as wrong)*, and second of all what does this have to do with the 70s, when I was a kid? By then life was completely different. I heard other arguments, like food shortages (again, not true, it's not like there was no food at all, there were shortages of this or that specific product, like you wouldn't find mayo or bologna in the store some days, but everything else was there!). So, you would come back next day, or in 2-3 days, and you would find them there. Really, this is such a big deal? Or you would have to stay in line to buy some other product, (ravioli for example). But how badly do you want that ravioli really that day, can't you have anything else instead? Just buy something else, like potatoes, where there was no line.

Was this annoying, yes, and at the time I was annoyed too, but only now I realized that I would much prefer this nuisance to my present life now, when I am constantly under stress for the fear that I can possibly lose my job (as my husband already did), and as a result, lose everything else – my house? You couldn't possibly lose your house in Soviet Union, it was yours for life, mortgage free. Only now, living here in the US, I realized that all those soviet nuisances combined were not as important as the benefits we had – housing, education, healthcare, employment, safe streets, all sort of free after school activities (music, sports, arts, anything you want) for kids, so parents never had to worry about what we do all day till they come home in the evening.

We've all heard the figures many times ... 10 million ... 20 million ... 40 million ... 60 million ... died under Stalin. But what does the number mean, whichever number you choose? Of course many people died under Stalin, many people died under Roosevelt, and many people are still dying under Bush. Dying appears to be a natural phenomenon in every country. The question is how did those people die under Stalin? Did they die from the famines that plagued the USSR in the 1920s and 30s? Did the Bolsheviks deliberately create those famines? How? Why? More people certainly died in India in the 20th century from famines than in the Soviet Union, but no one accuses India of the mass murder of its own citizens. Did the millions die from disease in an age before antibiotics? In prison? From what causes? People die in prison in the United States on a regular basis. Were millions actually murdered in cold blood? If so, how? How many were criminals executed for non-political crimes? The logistics of murdering tens of millions of people is daunting. (William Blum)[48]

Hungary

The following two stories from Hungary can be found on my blog, published in full, where I believe it constitutes a case of "fair use" for research and educational purposes. From my blog you can follow the link to the original source of the article if you like (if it's still there).

<u>Oppressive and grey? No, growing up under communism was the happiest time of my life</u>

<u>https://prolecenter.wordpress.com/2013/11/09/oppressive-and-grey-no-growing-up-under-communism-was-the-happiest-time-of-my-life-2/</u>

Goulash and Solidarity

https://prolecenter.wordpress.com/2014/08/26/goulash-and-solidarity/

Notes

<hr>

[1] Hearing on U.S. Security Strategy Post-9/11 Testimony before House Committee on Oversight and Government Reform November 6, 2007: http://www.hks.harvard.edu/news-events/news/testimonies/joseph-nye-testifies-before-congress-on-u.s.-security-strategy-post-9-11 (This webpage has since been removed.)

[2] It turns out that George Orwell was a reactionary snitch working with British Intelligence, but this statement of his still stands as a more or less accurate appraisal of right-wing libertarian foolishness. For more information consult this article on The Greanville Post: http://www.greanvillepost.com/2017/06/06/hard-awakenings-george-orwell-was-a-reactionary-snitch-who-made-a-blacklist-of-leftists-for-the-british-government/

The quote from Orwell's review of Hayek's book can be found on Wikiquote:

https://en.wikiquote.org/wiki/The_Road_to_Serfdom#Quotes_about_The_Road_to_Serfdom

[3] Mein Kampf (Murphy translation), p. 506; *http://greatwar.nl/books/meinkampf/meinkampf.pdf*)

[4] Wikipedia entry on "New World Order (conspiracy theory)"

[5] Wise, David and Ross, Thomas B. The Invisible Government. New York: Random House, 1964, pp. 346 – 7.

[6] MSN.com, "Trump, Clinton win big in NY, push closer to nomination" (Apparently, this webpage has also been removed.)

[7] Berlet, Chip and Lyons, Matthew N. Right-Wing Populism in America: Too Close For Comfort. New York: The Guilford Press, 2000.

[8] Rolling Stone magazine, Issue 75, Interview with John Lennon, February 4, 1971. Accessed via Jann S. Wenner's (Interviewer) website: http://www.jannswenner.com/archives/john_lennon_part2.aspx

[9] https://en.wikiquote.org/wiki/Joseph_Goebbels

[10] Email communications with Vltchek, Furr and Stewart in November 2014.

[11] Email communication with Andre Vltchek in November 2014.

[12] *https://www.bloomberg.com/view/articles/2017-11-03/in-defense-of-some-whataboutism*

[13] Wikipedia entry on "Doctor Zhivago (novel)"

[14] Finn, Peter and Couvée, Petra. "During Cold War, CIA used 'Doctor Zhivago' as a tool to undermine Soviet Union", The Washington Post, April 5, 2014.

[15] Ibid.

[16] Ibid.

[17] Finn, Op. Cit.; Carswell, Beth. "Giangiacomo Feltrinelli: The Revolutionary Publisher Who Saved Dr. Zhivago", AbeBooks.com, date not given.

[18] Jansen, S. Curry and Martin, Brian. "Exposing and opposing censorship: Backfire dynamics in freedom-of-speech struggles", Pacific Journalism Review, 2004, 10(1), 29-45.

[19] Ibid.

[20] Fox, Margalit, "Thomas P. Whitney, Solzhenitsyn Translator, Dies at 90", New York Times, December 12, 2007.

[21] Wikipedia entry on "Gulag"

[22] Thomas, D.M., Alexander Solzhenitsyn: A Century in His Life. St. Martin's Press: New York, 1998.

[23] *Great Hearts of Courage: Alexander Solzhenitsyn* (documentary), New Dimension Media, 2009.

[24] Ibid.

[25] Ibid.

[26] Thomas, Op. Cit.

[27] https://gowans.wordpress.com/2013/11/09/the-revolution-will-not-be-televised-nor-will-it-be-brought-to-you-by-russell-brand-oliver-stone-or-noam-chomsky/

[28] https://www.telegraph.co.uk/film/the-hunger-games-mockingjay-part-2/politics-protests-katniss-suzanne-collins/

[29] https://www.imdb.com/title/tt0091886/quotes/?tab=qt&ref_=tt_trv_qu

[30] https://www.theguardian.com/film/filmblog/2014/nov/14/why-on-screen-bad-guys-are-always-russian

[31] https://www.nytimes.com/2014/01/19/opinion/sunday/why-are-russians-still-the-go-to-bad-guys.html?_r=0

[32] *International Spy Museum Blog, "The Americans – Fact or Fiction?" http://blog.spymuseum.org/the-americans-fact-or-fiction/*

[33] *The Blaze, "Is TV's New Cold-War Spy Thriller Anti-American? Producer Admits 'We Want You to Root for the KGB.' http://www.theblaze.com/stories/2013/02/18/is-tvs-new-cold-war-spy-thriller-anti-american-producer-admits-we-want-you-to-root-for-the-kgb/*

[34] *Writer's Digest, "Defining and Developing Your Anti-Hero" http://www.writersdigest.com/qp7-migration-books/bullies_excerpt*

[35] https://en.wikipedia.org/wiki/COINTELPRO

[36] https://www.theguardian.com/uk-news/2014/oct/09/satanic-panic-british-agents-stoked-fears-troubles

[37] A sleeper agent is an intelligence asset put in place and not activated (put to use) for many years. This helps establish a firm cover.

[38] A Romeo agent seduces and establishes a romantic relationship with someone with access to intelligence or who might be used as a witting or unwitting agent of influence, sabotage, disruption or whatever.

[39] This was another hyperlink to a website that has also since been taken down. It was on Harvard's website, but for anyone who wants to do their homework, perhaps the full transcript of this hearing can be found in federal public records. And I thought censorship was just something those "other guys" did!

[40] Bennett, Jr., Lerone. Forced into Glory: Abraham Lincoln's White Dream. Chicago: Johnson Publishing Co., 2000.

[41] All quotes from Wikiquotes: https://en.wikiquote.org/wiki/Abraham_Lincoln

[42] https://www.mayoclinic.org/diseases-conditions/antisocial-personality-disorder/symptoms-causes/syc-20353928

[43] Marcuse, Peter. Missing Marx: A Personal and Political Journal of a Year in East Germany 1989 – 1990. New York: Monthly Review Press, 1991

[44] Ibid.

[45] Stalin's Moustache blog: https://stalinsmoustache.org/2015/12/16/bulgarian-joke-communism-is-back-in-power/

[46] Marcuse, Op. Cit.

[47] Ibid.

[48] Blum, William. The Anti-Empire Report #122: https://williamblum.org/aer/read/122